Air Fryer Cookbook for One

Practical Guide on How to Cook Your Favorite Foods Quickly and Healthy | Affordable and Delicious Recipes that Busy People Can Easily Prepare [Grey Edition]

By Brenda Roberts

TABLE OF CONTENTS

1. Introduction

This book was written with the purpose of helping owners (or future owners) of an air fryer to cook their favorite foods in a very healthy way.

We don't always have the time to devote to cooking food the traditional way; we have hectic lives, full of commitments and impossible schedules, so having an aid like an air fryer allows us to save time, without giving up the foods we love most.

Below are some of the benefits that the air fryer can bring to our lives:

It's safe to say that fried foods are frowned upon and many of us are eliminating them almost entirely from our diets. Those, however, who do not want to give up the classic crunchiness of chips and finger food are opting for an alternative, healthy and innovative method of cooking, that offered by oil-free fryers. Now extremely popular, these appliances have the reputation of being able to fry food by lowering the fat content. So let's find out how healthy these air fryers really are and what benefits they can offer.

- *Reduce the fat content of foods*

Fried foods are generally fattier than those prepared using other cooking methods. By making use of an air fryer, however, you can significantly reduce the calories contained in such foods by up to 75%.

This is because air fryers require much less oil than traditional fryers to achieve the same result. In fact, just think that while many recipes for fried dishes require up to 3 cups of oil, equal to 750 ml, those prepared in the air require only about 1 tablespoon, so 15 ml.

This means that traditional frying requires up to 50 times more oil, and while not all of the fat is actually absorbed by the food, what we ingest is still considered too harmful for our bodies.

This can have a big impact on your health, as higher fat intake from vegetable oils has been associated with increased heart disease and inflammation.

- *Real help in weight loss*

Being high in fat, fried foods contain more calories and, as a result, can contribute to weight gain.

So, if your goal is to lose a few extra inches on your waistline, then switching to an air fryer can be a good place to start. This is because since air-fried foods are less fatty than those prepared by traditional frying, opting for an air fryer can be an easy way to reduce calories and promote weight loss.

- *Less formation of harmful substances*

In addition to being higher in fat and calories, fried foods can create potentially dangerous and harmful health compounds that are formed during very high heat cooking methods, just like frying. Some of these substances, such as acrylamide, may be linked to the development of cancer.

Preferring air frying to traditional frying can help reduce the content of carcinogens in food.

- *Facilitating a healthier diet*

Although more studies are needed in this regard, in general it can be said that air-fried foods are much healthier than those cooked using different cooking methods. These are low in fat, calories and even some potentially harmful compounds found in traditionally fried foods.

So, to reduce our fat intake without changing or reducing what we love to eat the most, switching to an oil-free fryer can be a good choice for our health.

I hope this book will prove to be your best companion on your journey to healthy and tasty eating.

You will find easy-to-prepare recipes with simple ingredients that you can already find in your kitchen.

Always remember to consult the operating manual of your air fryer and adapt the instructions in the recipes to your needs.

AIR FRYER
BREAKFAST RECIPE

1) *Yummy Breakfast Italian Frittata*

Preparation Time: 5 minutes

Cooking Time: 0 minutes

Servings: 6

Nutrition: Calories 225 Fat 14g Carbs 4.5g Protein 20g

Ingredients:
- 6 eggs
- 1/3 cup of milk
- 4-ounces of chopped Italian sausage
- 3 cups of stemmed and roughly chopped kale
- 1 red deseeded and chopped bell pepper
- ½ cup of a grated feta cheese
- 1 chopped zucchini
- 1 tablespoon of freshly chopped basil
- 1 teaspoon of garlic powder
- 1 teaspoon of onion powder
- 1 teaspoon of salt
- 1 teaspoon of black pepper

Directions:
- ❖ Turn on the air fryer to 360 degrees Fahrenheit.
- ❖ Grease the air fryer pan with nonstick spray.
- ❖ Add the Italian sausage to the skillet and cook it in the air fryer for 5 minutes.
- ❖ While you're doing that, add and mix in the remaining ingredients until well combined.
- ❖ Add the egg mixture to the skillet and let it cook in the air fryer for 5 minutes.
- ❖ After that, carefully remove the pan and let it cool until cool enough to serve.
- ❖ Serve and enjoy!

2) *Savory Cheese and Bacon Muffins*

Preparation Time: 5 minutes

Cooking Time: 17 minutes

Servings: 4

Nutrition: Calories 180 Fat 18g Carbs 16g Protein 15g

Ingredients:
- 1 ½ cup of all-purpose flour
- 2 teaspoons of baking powder
- ½ cup of milk
- 2 eggs
- 1 tablespoon of freshly chopped parsley
- 4 cooked and chopped bacon slices
- 1 thinly chopped onion
- ½ cup of shredded cheddar cheese
- ½ teaspoon of onion powder
- 1 teaspoon of salt
- 1 teaspoon of black pepper

Directions:
- ❖ Turn on the fryer to 360 degrees Fahrenheit.
- ❖ Using a large bowl, add and mix all ingredients until well combined.
- ❖ Then grease muffin cups with non-stick cooking spray or line them with parchment paper. Pour the batter proportionally into each muffin cup.
- ❖ Place inside your air fryer and cook for 15 minutes.
- ❖ After that, carefully remove it from the fryer and let it cool.
- ❖ Serve and enjoy!

3) *Best Air-Fried English Breakfast*

Preparation Time: 5 minutes

Cooking Time: 20 minutes

Servings: 4

Nutrition: Calories 850 Fat 40g Carbs 20g Protein 48g

Ingredients:
- 8 sausages
- 8 bacon slices
- 4 eggs
- 1 (16-ounce) can of baked beans
- 8 slices of toast

Directions:
- ❖ Add the sausage and bacon slices to your air fryer and bake for 10 minutes at 320 degrees Fahrenheit.
- ❖ Using a heatproof ramekin or bowl, add the baked beans, then place another ramekin and add the eggs and whisk.
- ❖ Increase the temperature to 290 degrees Fahrenheit.
- ❖ Place inside your air fryer and bake for another 10 minutes or until all is done.
- ❖ Serve and enjoy!

4) _Sausage and Egg Breakfast Burrito_

Preparation Time: 5 minutes

Cooking Time: 30 minutes

Servings: 6

Nutrition: Calories 236 Fat 13g Carbs 16g Protein 15g

Ingredients:

- 6 eggs
- Salt
- Pepper
- Cooking oil
- ½ cup chopped red bell pepper
- ½ cup chopped green bell pepper
- 8 ounces ground chicken sausage
- ½ cup salsa
- 6 medium (8-inch) flour tortillas
- ½ cup shredded Cheddar cheese

Directions:

- ❖ In a medium bowl, beat eggs. Add salt and pepper to taste.
- ❖ Place a skillet over medium-high heat. Drizzle with cooking oil. Add eggs. Stir for 2 to 3 minutes, until eggs are foamy. Remove eggs from skillet and set aside.
- ❖ If necessary, spray the pan with more oil. Add the chopped red and green peppers. Cook for 2 to 3 minutes, when the peppers are soft.
- ❖ Add the ground sausage to the skillet. Break the sausage into smaller pieces using a spatula or spoon. Cook for 3 to 4 minutes, until the sausage is brown.
- ❖ Add the sauce and scrambled eggs. Stir to combine. Remove the pan from the heat.
- ❖ Spread the mixture evenly over the tortillas.
- ❖ To form burritos, fold the sides of each tortilla toward the center and then roll up from the bottom. You can secure each burrito with a toothpick. Or you can moisten the outside edge of the tortilla with a small amount of water. I prefer to use a kitchen brush, but you can also dab with your fingers.
- ❖ Spray the burritos with cooking oil and place them in the air fryer. Do not stack. Cook burritos in batches if they don't all fit in the basket. Cook for 8 minutes
- ❖ Open the air fryer and flip the burritos. Heat for an additional 2 minutes or until crispy.
- ❖ If necessary, repeat steps 8 and 9 for the remaining burritos.
- ❖ Sprinkle the burritos with the cheddar cheese. Cool before serving.

5) _French Toast Sticks_

Preparation Time: 5 minutes

Cooking Time: 15 minutes

Servings: 12

Nutrition: Calories 52 Fat 2g Carbs 7g Protein 2g

Ingredients:

- 4 slices Texas toast (or any thick bread, such as challah)
- 1 tablespoon butter
- 1 egg
- 1 teaspoon stevia
- 1 teaspoon ground cinnamon
- ¼ cup milk
- 1 teaspoon vanilla extract
- Cooking oil

Directions:

- ❖ Cut each slice of bread into 3 pieces (for a total of 12 sticks).
- ❖ Place the butter in a small microwave-safe bowl. Heat for 15 seconds, or until butter is melted.
- ❖ Remove the bowl from the microwave. Add the egg, stevia, cinnamon, milk and vanilla extract. Whisk until fully combined.
- ❖ Drizzle the fryer basket with cooking oil.
- ❖ Dip each of the bread sticks into the egg mixture.
- ❖ Place the French toast sticks in the fryer. It's okay to stack them. Drizzle the French toast sticks with cooking oil. Cook for 8 minutes
- ❖ Open the fryer and flip each French toast stick. Cook for an additional 4 minutes, or until French toast sticks are crispy.
- ❖ Cool before serving.

6) _Home-Fried Potatoes_

Preparation Time: 5 minutes

Cooking Time: 25 minutes

Servings: 4

Nutrition: Calories 279 Fat 8g Carbs 50g Protein 6g

Ingredients:
- 3 large russet potatoes
- 1 tablespoon canola oil
- 1 tablespoon extra-virgin olive oil
- 1 teaspoon paprika
- Salt
- Pepper
- 1 cup chopped onion
- 1 cup chopped red bell pepper
- 1 cup chopped green bell pepper

Directions:
- ❖ Cut the potatoes into 1/2-inch cubes. Place the potatoes in a large bowl of cold water and let them soak for at least 30 minutes, preferably an hour.
- ❖ Dry the potatoes and wipe them thoroughly with paper towels. Return them to the empty bowl.
- ❖ Add the canola and olive oils, paprika, and salt and pepper for flavor. Stir to completely coat the potatoes.
- ❖ Transfer the potatoes to the air fryer. Cook for 20 minutes, shaking the fryer basket every 5 minutes (a total of 4 times).
- ❖ Place the onion and red and green peppers in the fryer basket. Fry for another 3 to 4 minutes, or until potatoes are cooked and peppers are soft.
- ❖ Cool before serving.

7) _Homemade Cherry Breakfast Tarts_

Preparation Time: 15 minutes

Cooking Time: 20 minutes

Servings: 6

Nutrition: Calories 119 Fat 4g Carbs 19g Protein 2g

Ingredients:
- For the tarts:
- 2 refrigerated piecrusts
- ⅓ Cup cherry preserves
- 1 teaspoon cornstarch
- Cooking oil
- For the frosting:
- ½ cup vanilla yogurt
- 1-ounce cream cheese
- 1 teaspoon stevia
- Rainbow sprinkles

Directions:
- ❖ To make the tarts:
- ❖ Place the piecrusts on a flat surface. Make use of a knife or pizza cutter, cut each piecrust into 3 rectangles, for 6 in total. (I discard the unused dough left from slicing the edges.)
- ❖ In a small bowl, combine the preserves and cornstarch. Mix well.
- ❖ Scoop 1 tablespoon of the preserve mixture onto the top half of each piece of piecrust.
- ❖ Fold the bottom of each piece up to close the tart. Press along the edges of each tart to seal using the back of a fork.
- ❖ Sprinkle the breakfast tarts with cooking oil and place them in the air fryer. I do not recommend piling the breakfast tarts. They will stick together if piled. You may need to prepare them in two batches. Cook for 10 minutes
- ❖ Allow the breakfast tarts to cool fully before removing from the air fryer.
- ❖ If needed, repeat steps 5 and 6 for the remaining breakfast tarts.
- ❖ To make the frosting:
- ❖ In a small bowl, mix the yogurt, cream cheese, and stevia. Mix well.
- ❖ Spread the breakfast tarts with frosting and top with sprinkles, and serve.

8) _Sausage and Cream Cheese Biscuits_

Preparation Time: 5 minutes

Cooking Time: 15 minutes

Servings: 5

Nutrition: Calories 24g Fat 13g Carbs 20g Protein 9g

Ingredients:

- 12 ounces chicken breakfast sausage
- 1 (6-ounce) can biscuits
- ⅛ cup cream cheese

Directions:

- ❖ Form the sausage into 5 small patties.
- ❖ Place the sausage patties in the air fryer. Cook for 5 minutes.
- ❖ Open the air fryer. Flip the patties. Cook for another 5 minutes.
- ❖ Remove the cooked sausage patties from the fryer.
- ❖ Separate cookie dough into 5 cookies.
- ❖ Place the cookies in the fryer. Cook for 3 minutes
- ❖ Open the air fryer. Flip the cookies. Bake for another 2 minutes.
- ❖ Remove the cooked cookies from the fryer.
- ❖ Divide each cookie in half. Spread 1 teaspoon of cream cheese on the bottom of each cookie. Add a piece of sausage and the other half of the cookie and serve.

9) _Fried Chicken and Waffles_

Preparation Time: 10 minutes

Cooking Time: 30 minutes

Servings: 4

Nutrition: Calories 461 Fat 22g Carbs 45g Protein 28g

Ingredients:

- 8 whole chicken wings
- 1 teaspoon garlic powder
- Chicken seasoning or rub
- Pepper
- ½ cup all-purpose flour
- Cooking oil
- 8 frozen waffles
- Maple syrup (optional)

Directions:

- ❖ In a medium bowl, spice the chicken with the garlic powder and chicken seasoning and pepper for flavor.
- ❖ Place the chicken in a sealable plastic bag and add the flour. Shake to completely coat the chicken.
- ❖ Drizzle the fryer basket with cooking oil.
- ❖ Using tongs, place the chicken from the bag into the fryer. It's okay to stack the chicken wings on top of each other. Drizzle them with cooking oil. Heat for five minutes
- ❖ Unlock the air fryer and shake the basket. Presume to cook the chicken. Continue shaking every 5 minutes until 20 minutes have passed and the chicken is fully cooked.
- ❖ Remove the cooked chicken from the air fryer and set aside.
- ❖ Wash the basket and base with hot water. Return them to the air fryer.
- ❖ Increase the temperature of the fryer to 370°F.
- ❖ Place the frozen waffles in the fryer. Do not pile up. Depending on how big your air fryer is, you may need to cook the waffles in batches. Drizzle the waffles with cooking oil. Cook for 6 minutes
- ❖ If necessary, remove the cooked waffles from the fryer, then repeat step 9 for the remaining waffles.
- ❖ Serve the waffles with the chicken and a little maple syrup, if desired.

10) Cheesy Tater Tot Breakfast Bake

Preparation Time: 5 minutes

Cooking Time: 20 minutes

Servings: 4

Nutrition: Calories 518 Fat 30g Carbs 31g Protein 30g

Ingredients:

- 4 eggs
- 1 cup milk
- 1 teaspoon onion powder
- Salt
- Pepper
- Cooking oil
- 12 ounces ground chicken sausage
- 1-pound frozen tater tots
- ¾ cup shredded Cheddar cheese

Directions:

- ❖ In a medium bowl, whisk the eggs. Add the milk, onion powder, and salt and pepper to taste. Stir to combine.
- ❖ Spray a skillet with cooking oil and set over medium-high heat. Add the ground sausage. Using a spatula or spoon, break the sausage into smaller pieces. Cook for 3 to 4 minutes, until the sausage is brown. Remove from heat and set aside.
- ❖ Spray a barrel pan with cooking oil. Make sure to cover the bottom and sides of the pan.
- ❖ Place the tater tots in the barrel pan. Cook for 6 minutes
- ❖ Open the air fryer and shake the pan, then add the egg mixture and cooked sausage. Cook for an additional 6 minutes. Open the air fryer and sprinkle the cheese over the tater tot bake. Cook for an additional 2 to 3 minutes
- ❖ Cool before serving.

11) Breakfast Scramble Casserole

Preparation Time: 20 minutes

Cooking Time: 10 minutes

Servings: 4

Nutrition: Calories 348 Fat 26g Carbs 4g Protein 25g

Ingredients:

- 6 slices bacon
- 6 eggs
- Salt
- Pepper
- Cooking oil
- ½ cup chopped red bell pepper
- ½ cup chopped green bell pepper
- ½ cup chopped onion
- ¾ cup shredded Cheddar cheese

Directions:

- ❖ In a skillet, over medium-high heat, cook bacon, 5 to 7 minutes, turning to make it evenly crisp. Pat dry on paper towels, crumble and set aside.
- ❖ In a medium bowl, beat eggs. Add salt and pepper to taste.
- ❖ Spray a barrel pan with cooking oil. Be sure to cover the bottom and sides of the pan.
- ❖ Add the beaten eggs, crumbled bacon, red bell bell pepper, green bell bell pepper and onion to the skillet.
- ❖ Place the skillet in the air fryer. Cook for 6 minutes.
- ❖ Open the fryer and spread the cheese over the pan.
- ❖ Cook for an additional 2 minutes.
- ❖ Cool before serving.

12) Breakfast Grilled Ham and Cheese

Preparation Time: 5 minutes

Cooking Time: 10 minutes

Servings: 2

Nutrition: Calories 525 Fat 25g Carbs 34g Protein 41g

Ingredients:

- 1 teaspoon butter
- 4 slices bread
- 4 slices smoked country ham
- 4 slices Cheddar cheese
- 4 thick slices tomato

Directions:

- ❖ Spread ½ teaspoon of butter onto one side of 2 slices of bread. Each sandwich will have 1 slice of bread with butter and 1 slice without.
- ❖ Assemble each sandwich by layering 2 slices of ham, 2 slices of cheese, and 2 slices of tomato on the unbuttered pieces of bread. Top with the other bread slices, buttered side up.
- ❖ Place the sandwiches in the air fryer buttered-side down. Cook for 4 minutes
- ❖ Open the air fryer. Flip the grilled cheese sandwiches. Cook for an additional 4 minutes
- ❖ Cool before serving. Cut each sandwich in half and enjoy.

13) Classic Hash Browns

Preparation Time: 15 minutes

Cooking Time: 20 minutes

Servings: 4

Nutrition: Calories 150 Sodium: 52mg Carbs 34g Fiber 5g Protein 4g

Ingredients:

- 4 russet potatoes
- 1 teaspoon paprika
- Salt
- Pepper
- Cooking oil

Directions:

- ❖ Peel the potatoes using a vegetable peeler. Using a cheese grater shred the potatoes. If your grater has different-size holes, use the area of the tool with the largest holes.
- ❖ Put the shredded potatoes in a large bowl of cold water. Let sit for 5 minutes Cold water helps remove excess starch from the potatoes. Stir to help dissolve the starch.
- ❖ Dry out the potatoes and dry with paper towels or napkins. Make sure the potatoes are completely dry.
- ❖ Season the potatoes with the paprika and salt and pepper to taste.
- ❖ Spray the potatoes with cooking oil and transfer them to the air fryer. Cook for 20 minutes and shake the basket every 5 minutes (a total of 4 times).
- ❖ Cool before serving.

14) Canadian Bacon and Cheese English Muffins

Preparation Time: 5 minutes

Cooking Time: 10 minutes

Servings: 4

Nutrition: Calories 333 Fat 14g Carbs 27g Protein 24g

Ingredients:

- 4 English muffins
- 8 slices Canadian bacon
- 4 slices cheese
- Cooking oil

Directions:

- ❖ Split each English muffin. Assemble the breakfast sandwiches by layering 2 slices of Canadian bacon and 1 slice of cheese onto each English muffin bottom. Put the other half on top of the English muffin. Place the sandwiches in the air fryer. Spray the top of each with cooking oil. Cook for 4 minutes
- ❖ Open the air fryer and flip the sandwiches. Cook for an additional 4 minutes
- ❖ Cool before serving.

15) Radish Hash Browns

Preparation Time: 10 minutes

Cooking Time: 13 minutes

Servings: 4

Nutrition: Calories 62 Fat 3.7 g Carbs 7.1 g Protein 1.2 g

Ingredients:

- 1 lb. radishes, washed and cut off roots
- 1 tbsp olive oil
- 1/2 tsp paprika
- 1/2 tsp onion powder
- 1/2 tsp garlic powder
- 1 medium onion
- 1/4 tsp pepper
- 3/4 tsp sea salt

Directions:

- ❖ Slice onion and radishes using a mandolin slicer.
- ❖ Add sliced onion and radishes in a large mixing bowl and toss with olive oil.
- ❖ Transfer onion and radish slices in air fryer basket and cook at 360 F for 8 minutes Shake basket twice.
- ❖ Return onion and radish slices in a mixing bowl and toss with seasonings.
- ❖ Again, cook onion and radish slices in air fryer basket for 5 minutes at 400 F. Shake the basket halfway through.
- ❖ Serve and enjoy.

16) Vegetable Egg Cups

Preparation Time: 10 minutes

Cooking Time: 20 minutes

Servings: 4

Nutrition: Calories 194 Fat 11.5 g Carbs 6 g Protein 13 g

Ingredients:

-
- 4 eggs
- 1 tbsp cilantro, chopped
- 4 tbsp half and half
- 1 cup cheddar cheese, shredded
- 1 cup vegetables, diced
- Pepper
- Salt

Directions:

- ❖ Sprinkle four ramekins with cooking spray and set aside.
- ❖ In a mixing bowl, beat eggs with cilantro, half-and-half, vegetables, 1/2 cup cheese, pepper and salt.
- ❖ Pour the egg mixture into the four ramekins.
- ❖ Place ramekins in basket of deep fryer and bake at 300 F for 12 minutes
- ❖ Top with remaining 1/2 cup cheese and bake for 2 more minutes at 400 F.
- ❖ Serve and enjoy.

17) *Spinach Frittata*

Preparation Time: 5 minutes

Cooking Time: 8 minutes

Servings: 1

Nutrition: Calories 384 Fat 23.3 g Carbs 10.7 g Protein 34.3 g

Ingredients:
- 3 eggs
- 1 cup spinach, chopped
- 1 small onion, minced
- 2 tbsp mozzarella cheese, grated
- Pepper
- Salt

Directions:
- ❖ Preheat the air fryer to 350 F. Spray air fryer pan with cooking spray.
- ❖ In a bowl, whisk eggs with remaining ingredients until well combined.
- ❖ Pour egg mixture into the prepared pan and place pan in the air fryer basket.
- ❖ Cook frittata for 8 minutes or until set. Serve and enjoy.

18) *Omelet Frittata*

Preparation Time: 10 minutes

Cooking Time: 6 minutes

Servings: 2

Nutrition: Calories 160 Fat 10 g Carbs 4 g Protein 12 g

Ingredients:
- 3 eggs, lightly beaten
- 2 tbsp cheddar cheese, shredded
- 2 tbsp heavy cream
- 2 mushrooms, sliced
- 1/4 small onion, chopped
- 1/4 bell pepper, diced
- Pepper
- Salt

Directions:
- ❖ In a bowl, whisk eggs with cream, vegetables, pepper, and salt.
- ❖ Preheat the air fryer to 400 F.
- ❖ Pour egg mixture into the air fryer pan. Place pan in air fryer basket and cook for 5 minutes
- ❖ Add shredded cheese on top of the frittata and cook for 1 minute more.
- ❖ Serve and enjoy.

19) *Cheese Soufflés*

Preparation Time: 10 minutes

Cooking Time: 6 minutes

Servings: 8

Nutrition: Calories 210 Fat 16 g Carbs 1 g Protein 12 g

Ingredients:
- 6 large eggs, separated
- 3/4 cup heavy cream
- 1/4 tsp cayenne pepper
- 1/2 tsp xanthan gum
- 1/2 tsp pepper
- 1/4 tsp cream of tartar
- 2 tbsp chives, chopped
- 2 cups cheddar cheese, shredded
- 1 tsp salt

Directions:
- ❖ Preheat the air fryer to 325 F.
- ❖ Spray eight ramekins with cooking spray. Set aside.
- ❖ In a bowl, whisk together almond flour, cayenne pepper, pepper, salt, and xanthan gum.
- ❖ Slowly add heavy cream and mix to combine.
- ❖ Whisk in egg yolks, chives, and cheese until well combined.
- ❖ In a large bowl, add egg whites and cream of tartar and beat until stiff peaks form.
- ❖ Fold egg white mixture into the almond flour mixture until combined.
- ❖ Pour mixture into the prepared ramekins. Divide ramekins in batches.
- ❖ Place the first batch of ramekins into the air fryer basket.
- ❖ Cook soufflé for 20 minutes
- ❖ Serve and enjoy.

20) *Simple Egg Soufflé*

Preparation Time: 5 minutes

Cooking Time: 8 minutes

Servings: 2

Nutrition: Calories 116 Fat 10 g Carbs 1.1 g Protein 6 g

Ingredients:
- 2 eggs
- 1/4 tsp chili pepper
- 2 tbsp heavy cream
- 1/4 tsp pepper
- 1 tbsp parsley, chopped
- Salt

Directions:
- ❖ In a bowl, whisk eggs with remaining gradients.
- ❖ Spray two ramekins with cooking spray.
- ❖ Pour egg mixture into the prepared ramekins and place into the air fryer basket.
- ❖ Cook soufflé at 390 F for 8 minutes
- ❖ Serve and enjoy.

21) Vegetable Egg Soufflé

Preparation Time: 10 minutes

Cooking Time: 20 minutes

Servings: 4

Nutrition: Calories 91 Fat 5.1 g Carbs 4.7 g Protein 7.4 g

Ingredients:

-
- 4 large eggs
- 1 tsp onion powder
- 1 tsp garlic powder
- 1 tsp red pepper, crushed
- 1/2 cup broccoli florets, chopped
- 1/2 cup mushrooms, chopped

Directions:

- ❖ Sprinkle four ramekins with cooking spray and set aside.
- ❖ In a bowl, whisk eggs with onion powder, garlic powder, and red pepper.
- ❖ Add mushrooms and broccoli and stir well.
- ❖ Pour egg mixture into the prepared ramekins and place ramekins into the air fryer basket.
- ❖ Cook at 350 F for 15 minutes Make sure soufflé is cooked if soufflé is not cooked then cook for 5 minutes more.
- ❖ Serve and enjoy.

22) Asparagus Frittata

Preparation Time:

Cooking Time:

Servings:

Nutrition: Calories 211 Fat 13 g Carbs 4 g Protein 16 g

Ingredients:

- 6 eggs
- 3 mushrooms, sliced
- 10 asparagus, chopped
- 1/4 cup half and half
- 2 tsp butter, melted
- 1 cup mozzarella cheese, shredded
- 1 tsp pepper
- 1 tsp salt

Directions:

- ❖ Toss mushrooms and asparagus with melted butter and add into the air fryer basket. Cook mushrooms and asparagus at 350 F for 5 minutes Shake basket twice.
- ❖ Meanwhile, in a bowl, whisk together eggs, half and half, pepper, and salt. Transfer cook mushrooms and asparagus into the air fryer baking dish. Pour egg mixture over mushrooms and asparagus.
- ❖ Place dish in the air fryer and cook at 350 F for 5 minutes or until eggs are set. Slice and serve.

23) Spicy Cauliflower Rice

Preparation Time: 10 minutes

Cooking Time: 22 minutes

Servings: 2

Nutrition: Calories 254 Fat 28 g Carbs 12.3 g Protein 4.3 g

Ingredients:

- 1 cauliflower head, cut into florets
- 1/2 tsp cumin
- 1/2 tsp chili powder
- 6 onion spring, chopped
- 2 jalapenos, chopped
- 4 tbsp olive oil
- 1 zucchini, trimmed and cut into cubes
- 1/2 tsp paprika
- 1/2 tsp garlic powder
- 1/2 tsp cayenne pepper
- 1/2 tsp pepper
- 1/2 tsp salt

Directions:

- ❖ Preheat the air fryer to 370 F.
- ❖ Add cauliflower florets into the food processor and process until it looks like rice.
- ❖ Transfer cauliflower rice into the air fryer baking pan and Drizzle with half oil.
- ❖ Place pan in the air fryer and cook for 12 minutes, stir halfway through.
- ❖ Heat the remaining oil in a small pan over medium heat.
- ❖ Add zucchini and cook for 5-8 minutes
- ❖ Add onion and jalapenos and cook for 5 minutes
- ❖ Add spices and stir well. Set aside.
- ❖ Add cauliflower rice in the zucchini mixture and stir well.
- ❖ Serve and enjoy.

24) Broccoli Stuffed Peppers

Preparation Time: 10 minutes

Cooking Time: 40 minutes

Servings: 2

Nutrition: Calories 340 Fat 22 g Carbs 12 g Protein 22 g

Ingredients:

- 4 eggs
- 1/2 cup cheddar cheese, grated
- 2 bell peppers cut in half and remove seeds
- 1/2 tsp garlic powder
- 1 tsp dried thyme
- 1/4 cup feta cheese, crumbled
- 1/2 cup broccoli, cooked
- 1/4 tsp pepper
- 1/2 tsp salt

Directions:

- ❖ Preheat the air fryer to 325 F.
- ❖ Stuff feta and broccoli into the bell peppers halved.
- ❖ Beat egg in a bowl with seasoning and pour egg mixture into the pepper halved over feta and broccoli.
- ❖ Place bell pepper halved into the air fryer basket and cook for 35-40 minutes
- ❖ Top with grated cheddar cheese and cook until cheese melted.
- ❖ Serve and enjoy.

25) Zucchini Muffins

Preparation Time: 10 minutes

Cooking Time: 20 minutes

Servings: 8

Nutrition: Calories 136 Fat 12 g Carbs 1 g Protein 4 g

Ingredients:

- 6 eggs
- 4 drops stevia
- 1/4 cup Swerve
- 1/3 cup coconut oil, melted
- 1 cup zucchini, grated
- 3/4 cup coconut flour
- 1/4 tsp ground nutmeg
- 1 tsp ground cinnamon
- 1/2 tsp baking soda

Directions:

- ❖ Preheat the air fryer to 325 F.
- ❖ Add all ingredients except zucchini in a bowl and mix well.
- ❖ Add zucchini and stir well.
- ❖ Pour batter into the silicone muffin molds and place into the air fryer basket.
- ❖ Cook muffins for 20 minutes
- ❖ Serve and enjoy.

26) alapeno Breakfast Muffins

Preparation Time: 10 minutes

Cooking Time: 15 minutes

Servings: 8

Nutrition: Calories 125 Fat 12 g Carbs 7 g Protein 3 g

Ingredients:

- 5 eggs
- 1/3 cup coconut oil, melted
- 2 tsp baking powder
- 3 tbsp erythritol
- 3 tbsp jalapenos, sliced
- 1/4 cup unsweetened coconut milk
- 2/3 cup coconut flour
- 3/4 tsp sea salt

Directions:

- ❖ Preheat the air fryer to 325 F.
- ❖ In a large bowl, mix together coconut flour, baking powder, erythritol, and sea salt.
- ❖ Stir in eggs, jalapenos, coconut milk, and coconut oil until well combined.
- ❖ Pour batter into the silicone muffin molds and place into the air fryer basket.
- ❖ Cook muffins for 15 minutes
- ❖ Serve and enjoy.

27) Zucchini Noodles

Preparation Time: 10 minutes

Cooking Time: 44 minutes

Servings: 3

Nutrition: Calories 435 Fat 29 g Carbs 10.4 g Protein 25 g

Ingredients:

- 1 egg
- 1/2 cup parmesan cheese, grated
- 1/2 cup feta cheese, crumbled
- 1 tbsp thyme
- 1 garlic clove, chopped
- 1 onion, chopped
- 2 medium zucchinis, trimmed and spiralized
- 2 tbsp olive oil
- 1 cup mozzarella cheese, grated
- 1/2 tsp pepper
- 1/2 tsp salt

Directions:

- ❖ Preheat the air fryer to 350 F.
- ❖ Add spiralized zucchini and salt in a colander and set aside for 10 minutes. Wash zucchini noodles and pat dry with a paper towel.
- ❖ Heat the oil in a pan over medium heat. Add garlic and onion and sauté for 3-4 minutes
- ❖ Add zucchini noodles and cook for 4-5 minutes or until softened.
- ❖ Add zucchini mixture into the air fryer baking pan. Add egg, thyme, cheeses. Mix well and season.
- ❖ Place pan in the air fryer and cook for 30-35 minutes
- ❖ Serve and enjoy.

28) Mushroom Frittata

Preparation Time: 10 minutes

Cooking Time: 13 minutes

Servings: 1

Nutrition: Calories 176 Fat 3 g Carbs 4 g Protein 31 g

Ingredients:
- 1 cup egg whites
- 1 cup spinach, chopped
- 2 mushrooms, sliced
- 2 tbsp parmesan cheese, grated
- Salt

Directions:
- ❖ Sprinkle pan with cooking spray and heat over medium heat. Add mushrooms and sauté for 2-3 minutes Add spinach and cook for 1-2 minutes or until wilted.
- ❖ Transfer mushroom spinach mixture into the air fryer pan. Beat egg whites in a mixing bowl until frothy. Season it with a pinch of salt.
- ❖ Pour egg white mixture into the spinach and mushroom mixture and sprinkle with parmesan cheese. Place pan in air fryer basket and cook frittata at 350 F for 8 minutes
- ❖ Slice and serve.

29) Egg Muffins

Preparation Time: 10 minutes

Cooking Time: 15 minutes

Servings: 12

Nutrition: Calories 135 Fat 11 g Carbs 1.5 g Protein 8 g

Ingredients:
- 9 eggs
- 1/2 cup onion, sliced
- 1 tbsp olive oil
- 8 oz ground sausage
- 1/4 cup coconut milk
- 1/2 tsp oregano
- 1 1/2 cups spinach
- 3/4 cup bell peppers, chopped
- Pepper
- Salt

Directions:
- ❖ Preheat the air fryer to 325 F.
- ❖ Add ground sausage in a pan and sauté over medium heat for 5 minutes
- ❖ Add olive oil, oregano, bell pepper, and onion and sauté until onion is translucent.
- ❖ Put spinach to the pan and cook for 30 seconds.
- ❖ Remove pan from heat and set aside.
- ❖ In a mixing bowl, whisk together eggs, coconut milk, pepper, and salt until well beaten.
- ❖ Add sausage and vegetable mixture into the egg mixture and mix well.
- ❖ Pour egg mixture into the silicone muffin molds and place into the air fryer basket. (Cook in batches)
- ❖ Cook muffins for 15 minutes
- ❖ Serve and enjoy.

30) Blueberry Breakfast Cobbler

Preparation Time: 5 minutes

Cooking Time: 15 minutes

Servings: 4

Nutrition: Calories 112 Fat 1g Carbs 23g Protein 3g

Ingredients:
- ⅓ cup whole-wheat pastry flour
- ¾ teaspoon baking powder
- Dash sea salt
- ½ cup 2% milk
- 2 tablespoons pure maple syrup
- ½ teaspoon vanilla extract
- Cooking oil spray
- ½ cup fresh blueberries
- ¼ cup Granola, or plain store-bought granola

Directions:
- ❖ In a medium bowl, whisk the flour, baking powder, and salt. Add the milk, maple syrup, and vanilla and gently whisk, just until thoroughly combined.
- ❖ Preheat the unit by selecting BAKE, setting the temperature to 350°F, and setting the time to 3 minutes Select START/STOP to start.
- ❖ Spray a 6-by-2-inch round baking pan with cooking oil and pour the batter into the pan. Top evenly with the blueberries and granola.
- ❖ Once the unit is preheated, place the pan into the basket.
- ❖ Select BAKE, set the temperature to 350°F, and set the time to 15 minutes Select START/STOP to begin.
- ❖ When the cooking is complete, the cobbler should be nicely browned and a knife inserted into the middle should come out clean. Enjoy plain or topped with a little vanilla yogurt.

31) Homemade Strawberry Breakfast Tarts

Preparation Time: 15 minutes

Cooking Time: 20 minutes

Servings: 6

Nutrition: Calories 408 Fat 20.5g Carbs 56g Protein 1g

Ingredients:

- 2 refrigerated piecrusts
- ½ cup strawberry preserves
- 1 teaspoon cornstarch
- Cooking oil spray
- ½ cup low-fat vanilla yogurt
- 1-ounce cream cheese, at room temperature
- 3 tablespoons confectioners' sugar
- Rainbow sprinkles, for decorating

Directions:

❖ Place the piecrusts on a flat surface. Cut each piecrust into 3 rectangles using a knife or pizza cutter, for a total of 6. Discard any unused dough from the edges of the tart.

❖ In a small bowl, mix together the preserves and cornstarch. Mix well, making sure there are no lumps of cornstarch remaining.

❖ Place 1 tablespoon of the strawberry mixture on the top half of each tart piece.

❖ Fold the bottom of each piece upward to enclose the filling. Press along the edges of each tart to seal using the back of a fork.

❖ Insert the crisper plate into the basket and the basket into the unit. Preheat the unit by selecting bake, setting the temperature to 375°F and setting the time to 3 minutes Select start/stop to begin.

❖ Once the unit is preheated, spray the crisper plate with cooking oil. Working in batches, spray the breakfast tarts with cooking oil and place them in the basket in a single layer. Do not stack the tarts.

❖ Select bake, set temperature to 375°F and set time to 10 minutes Select start/stop to begin.

❖ When baking is complete, the tarts should be lightly browned. Allow the breakfast tarts to cool completely before removing them from the basket.

❖ Repeat steps 5, 6, 7 and 8 for the remaining breakfast tarts.

❖ In a small bowl, mix together the yogurt, cream cheese and powdered sugar. Spread the breakfast tarts with the frosting and top with the sprinkles.

32) Everything Bagels

Preparation Time: 10 minutes

Cooking Time: 10 minutes

Servings: 2

Nutrition: Calories 271 Fat 13g Carbs 28g Protein 10g

Ingredients:

- ½ cup self-rising flour, plus more for dusting
- ½ cup plain Greek yogurt
- 1 egg
- 1 tablespoon water
- 4 teaspoons everything bagel spice mix
- Cooking oil spray
- 1 tablespoon butter, melted

Directions:

❖ In a large bowl, using a wooden spoon, stir together the flour and yogurt until a tacky dough forms. Transfer the dough to a lightly floured work surface and roll the dough into a ball.

❖ Cut the dough into 2 pieces and roll each piece into a log. Form each log into a bagel shape, pinching the ends together.

❖ In a small bowl, whisk the egg and water. Brush the egg wash on the bagels.

❖ Sprinkle 2 teaspoons of the spice mix on each bagel and gently press it into the dough.

❖ Insert the crisper plate into the basket and the basket into the unit. Preheat the unit by selecting bake, setting the temperature to 330°F, and setting the time to 3 minutes Select start/stop to begin.

❖ Once the unit is preheated, spray the crisper plate with cooking spray. Drizzle with the bagels with the butter and place them into the basket.

❖ Select BAKE, set the temperature to 330°F, and set the time to 10 minutes Select START/STOP to begin.

❖ When the cooking is complete, the bagels should be lightly golden on the outside. Serve warm.

33) Easy Maple-Glazed Doughnuts

Preparation Time: 10 minutes

Cooking Time: 14 minutes

Servings: 8

Nutrition: Calories 219 Fat 10g Carbs 30g Protein 2g

Ingredients:

- 1 (8-count) can jumbo flaky refrigerator biscuits
- Cooking oil spray
- ½ cup light brown sugar
- ¼ cup butter
- 3 tablespoons milk
- 2 cups confectioners' sugar, plus more for dusting (optional)
- 2 teaspoons pure maple syrup

Directions:

- ❖ Insert the crisper plate into the basket and the basket into the unit. Preheat the unit by selecting air fry, setting the temperature to 350°F, and setting the time to 3 minutes Select start/stop to begin.
- ❖ Remove the biscuits from the tube and cut out the center of each biscuit with a small, round cookie cutter.
- ❖ Once the unit is preheated, spray the crisper plate with cooking oil. Work it in batches, place 4 doughnuts into the basket.
- ❖ Select air fry, set the temperature to 350°F, and set the time to 5 minutes Select start/stop to begin.
- ❖ When the cooking is complete, place the doughnuts on a plate. Repeat steps 3 and 4 with the remaining doughnuts.
- ❖ In a small saucepan over medium heat, combine the brown sugar, butter, and milk. Heat until the butter is melted and the sugar is dissolved, about 4 minutes
- ❖ Remove the pan from the heat and whisk in the confectioners' sugar and maple syrup until smooth.
- ❖ Dip the slightly cooled doughnuts into the maple glaze. Place them on a wire rack and dust with confectioners' sugar (if using). Let rest just until the glaze sets. Enjoy the doughnuts warm.

34) Chocolate-Filled Doughnut Holes

Preparation Time: 10 minutes

Cooking Time: 30 minutes

Servings: 12

Nutrition: Calories 393 Fat 17g Carbs 55g Protein 5g

Ingredients:

- 1 (8-count) can refrigerated biscuits
- Cooking oil spray
- 48 semisweet chocolate chips
- 3 tablespoons melted unsalted butter
- ¼ cup confectioners' sugar

Directions:

- ❖ Separate the cookies and cut each cookie into thirds, for 24 pieces.
- ❖ Flatten each cookie piece slightly and place 2 chocolate chips in the center.
- ❖ Wrap dough around chocolate and seal edges tightly.
- ❖ Insert the crisper plate into the basket and the basket into the unit.
- ❖ Preheat the unit by selecting air fry, setting the temperature to 330°F, and setting the time to 3 minutes Select start/stop to begin.
- ❖ Once the unit is preheated, spray the crisper plate with cooking oil.
- ❖ Brush each donut hole with a little butter and place in the basket.
- ❖ Select air frying, set the temperature to 330°F and set the time between 8 and 12 minutes Select start/stop to begin.
- ❖ The donuts are ready when they are golden brown.
- ❖ When cooking is complete, place donut holes on a plate and sprinkle with powdered sugar.
- ❖ Serve warm.

35) Delicious Original Hash Browns

Preparation Time: 15 minutes

Cooking Time: 20 minutes

Servings: 4

Nutrition: Calories 150 Fat 0g Carbs 34g Protein 4g

Ingredients:

- 4 russet potatoes, peeled
- 1 teaspoon paprika
- Salt
- Freshly ground black pepper
- Cooking oil spray

Directions:

- ❖ Using a box grater or food processor, shred the potatoes. If your grater has different hole sizes, use the largest holes.
- ❖ Place the shredded potatoes in a large bowl of cold water. Let it sit for 5 minutes (Cold water helps remove excess starch from the potatoes.) Stir them to help dissolve the starch.
- ❖ Insert the crisper plate into the basket and the basket into the unit. Preheat the unit by selecting air fry, setting the temperature to 360°F, and setting the time to 3 minutes Select start/stop to begin.
- ❖ Dry out the potatoes and pat them with paper towels until the potatoes are completely dry. Season the potatoes with the paprika, salt, and pepper.
- ❖ Once the unit is preheated, spray the crisper plate with cooking oil. Spray the potatoes with the cooking oil and place them into the basket.
- ❖ Select air fry, set the temperature to 360°F, and set the time to 20 minutes Select start/stop to begin.
- ❖ After 5 minutes, remove the basket and shake the potatoes. Reinsert the basket to resume cooking. Continue shaking the basket every 5 minutes (a total of 4 times) until the potatoes are done.
- ❖ When the cooking is complete, remove the hash browns from the basket and serve warm.

36) Puffed Egg Tarts

Preparation Time: 10 minutes

Cooking Time: 20 minutes

Servings: 4

Nutrition: Calories 322 Fat 24g Carbs 12g Protein 15g

Ingredients:

- ⅓Sheet frozen puff pastry, thawed
- Cooking oil spray
- ½ cup shredded Cheddar cheese
- 2 eggs
- ¼ teaspoon salt, divided
- 1 teaspoon minced fresh parsley (optional)

Directions:

- ❖ Insert the crisper plate into the basket and the basket into the unit. Preheat the unit by selecting bake, setting the temperature to 390°F, and setting the time to 3 minutes Select start/stop to begin.
- ❖ Lay the puff pastry sheet on a piece of parchment paper and cut it in half.
- ❖ Once the unit is preheated, spray the crisper plate with cooking oil. Transfer the 2 squares of pastry to the basket, keeping them on the parchment paper.
- ❖ Select bake, set the temperature to 390°F, and set the time to 20 minutes Select start/stop to begin.
- ❖ After 10 minutes, use a metal spoon to press down the center of each pastry square to make a well. Divide the cheese equally between the baked pastries. Carefully crack an egg on top of the cheese, and sprinkle each with the salt. Resume cooking for 7 to 10 minutes
- ❖ When the cooking is complete, the eggs will be cooked through. Sprinkle each with parsley (if using) and serve.

37) Early Morning Steak and Eggs

Preparation Time: 10 minutes

Cooking Time: 30 minutes

Servings: 4

Nutrition: Calories 304 Fat 19g Carbs 2g Protein 31g

Ingredients:

- Cooking oil spray
- 4 (4-ounce) New York strip steaks
- 1 teaspoon granulated garlic, divided
- 1 teaspoon salt, divided
- 1 teaspoon freshly ground black pepper, divided
- 4 eggs
- ½ teaspoon paprika

Directions:

- ❖ Insert the crisper plate into the basket and the basket into the unit. Preheat the unit by selecting air fry, setting the temperature to 360°F, and setting the time to 3 minutes Select start/stop to begin.
- ❖ Once the unit is preheated, spray the crisp dish with cooking oil. Place 2 steaks in the basket; do not oil or season them at this time.
- ❖ Select air frying, set temperature to 360°F and set time to 9 minutes Select start/stop to begin.
- ❖ After 5 minutes, open the unit and flip the steaks. Sprinkle each with ¼ teaspoon granulated garlic, ¼ teaspoon salt and ¼ teaspoon pepper. Resume cooking until the steaks register at least 145°F on a food thermometer.
- ❖ When cooking is complete, transfer steaks to a plate and cover with aluminum foil to keep warm. Repeat steps 2, 3 and 4 with remaining steaks.
- ❖ Drizzle 4 ramekins with olive oil. Crack 1 egg into each ramekin. Sprinkle eggs with paprika and remaining ½ teaspoon salt and pepper. Working in batches, place 2 ramekins in the basket.
- ❖ Select BAKE, set temperature to 330°F and set time to 5 minutes Select start/stop to begin. When cooking is complete and eggs are cooked to 160°F, remove ramekins and repeat step 7 with remaining 2 ramekins.
- ❖ Serve the eggs with the steaks.

38) Breakfast Potatoes

Preparation Time: 10 minutes

Cooking Time: 20 minutes

Servings: 6

Nutrition: Calories 199 Fat 1g Carbs 43g Protein 5g

Ingredients:

- 1½ teaspoons olive oil, divided, plus more for misting
- 4 large potatoes, skins on, cut into cubes
- 2 teaspoons seasoned salt, divided
- 1 teaspoon minced garlic, divided
- 2 large green or red bell peppers, cut into 1-inch chunks
- ½ onion, diced

Directions:

- ❖ Lightly mist the fryer basket with olive oil.
- ❖ In a medium bowl, toss the potatoes with ½ teaspoon of olive oil. Sprinkle with 1 teaspoon of seasoned salt and ½ teaspoon of minced garlic. Stir to coat.
- ❖ Place the seasoned potatoes in the fryer basket in a single layer.
- ❖ Cook for 5 minutes Shake the basket and cook for another 5 minutes
- ❖ Meanwhile, in a medium bowl, toss the bell peppers and onion with the remaining ½ teaspoon of olive oil.
- ❖ Sprinkle the peppers and onions with the remaining 1 teaspoon of seasoned salt and ½ teaspoon of minced garlic. Stir to coat.
- ❖ Add the seasoned peppers and onions to the fryer basket with the potatoes.
- ❖ Cook for 5 minutes Shake the basket and cook for an additional 5 minutes

39) Baked Potato Breakfast Boats

Preparation Time: 10 minutes

Cooking Time: 20 minutes

Servings: 4

Nutrition: Calories 338 Fat15g Saturated Fat 8g Cholesterol 214mg Carbs 35g Protein 17g Fiber 3g Sodium: 301mg

Ingredients:
- 2 large russet potatoes, scrubbed
- Olive oil
- Salt
- Freshly ground black pepper
- 4 eggs
- 2 tablespoons chopped, cooked bacon
- 1 cup shredded cheddar cheese

Directions:
- ❖ Poke holes in the potatoes with a fork and microwave on full power for 5 minutes. Turn potatoes over and cook an additional 3 to 5 minutes, or until the potatoes are fork tender.
- ❖ Cut the potatoes in half lengthwise and use a spoon to scoop out the inside of the potato. Be careful to leave a layer of potato so that it makes a sturdy "boat."Lightly spray the fryer basket with olive oil. Spray the skin side of the potatoes with oil and sprinkle with salt and pepper to taste.
- ❖ Place the potato skins in the fryer basket skin side down. Crack one egg into each potato skin.
- ❖ Sprinkle ½ tablespoon of bacon pieces and ¼ cup of shredded cheese on top of each egg. Sprinkle with salt and pepper to taste.
- ❖ Air fry until the yolk is slightly runny, 5 to 6 minutes, or until the yolk is fully cooked, 7 to 10 minutes

40) Greek Frittata

Preparation Time: 10 minutes

Cooking Time: 20 minutes

Servings: 4

Nutrition: Calories 146 Fat 10g Saturated Fat 5g Cholesterol 249mg Carbs 3g Protein 11g Fiber 1g Sodium: 454mg

Ingredients:
- Olive oil
- 5 eggs
- ¼ teaspoon salt
- ⅛ Teaspoon freshly ground black pepper
- 1 cup baby spinach leaves, shredded
- ½ cup halved grape tomatoes
- ½ cup crumbled feta cheese

Directions:
- ❖ Spray a small round air fryer pan with olive oil.
- ❖ In a medium bowl, whisk together eggs, salt and pepper and beat to combine.
- ❖ Add spinach and stir to combine.
- ❖ Pour ½ cup of the egg mixture into the skillet.
- ❖ Sprinkle ¼ cup of the tomatoes and ¼ cup of the feta cheese on top of the egg mixture.
- ❖ Cover the pan with aluminum foil and secure around the edges.
- ❖ Carefully place the pan in the basket of the fryer.
- ❖ Air fry for 12 minutes
- ❖ Remove foil from pan and cook until eggs are set, 5 to 7 minutes
- ❖ Remove omelet from pan and place on a serving platter. Repeat with remaining ingredients.

41) Mini Shrimp Frittata

Preparation Time: 15 minutes

Cooking Time: 20 minutes

Servings: 4

Nutrition: Calories 114 Fat 7g Carbs 1g Protein 12g

Ingredients:

- 1 teaspoon olive oil, plus more for spraying
- ½ small red bell pepper, finely diced
- 1 teaspoon minced garlic
- 1 (4-ounce) can of tiny shrimp, Dry out
- Salt
- Freshly ground black pepper
- 4 eggs, beaten
- 4 teaspoons ricotta cheese

Directions:

❖ Spray four ramekins with olive oil. In a medium skillet over medium-low heat, heat 1 teaspoon of olive oil. Add the bell pepper and garlic and sauté until the pepper is soft, about 5 minutes

❖ Add the shrimp, season with salt and pepper, and cook until warm, 1 to 2 minutes Remove from the heat.

❖ Add the eggs and stir to combine. Pour one quarter of the mixture into each ramekin.

❖ Place 2 ramekins in the fryer basket and cook for 6 minutes. Remove the fryer basket from the air fryer and stir the mixture in each ramekin. Top each frittata with 1 teaspoon of ricotta cheese. Return the fryer basket to the air fryer and cook until eggs are set and the top is lightly browned, 4 to 5 minutes

❖ Repeat with the remaining two ramekins.

42) Spinach and Mushroom Mini Quiche

Preparation Time: 10 minutes

Cooking Time: 15 minutes

Servings: 4

Nutrition: Calories 183 Fat 13g Saturated Fat 7g Cholesterol 206mg Carbs 3g Protein 14g Fiber 1g Sodium: 411mg

Ingredients:

- 1 teaspoon olive oil, plus more for spraying
- 1 cup coarsely chopped mushrooms
- 1 cup fresh baby spinach, shredded
- 4 eggs, beaten
- ½ cup shredded Cheddar cheese
- ½ cup shredded mozzarella cheese
- ¼ teaspoon salt
- ¼ teaspoon black pepper

Directions:

❖ Spray 4 silicone baking cups with olive oil and set aside. In a medium skillet over medium heat, heat 1 teaspoon olive oil. Add mushrooms and sauté until soft, 3 to 4 minutes

❖ Add spinach and cook until wilted, 1 to 2 minutes.

❖ In a medium bowl, whisk together the eggs, Cheddar cheese, mozzarella cheese, salt and pepper. Gently add the mushrooms and spinach to the egg mixture.

❖ Pour ¼ of the mixture into each silicone baking cup. Place the baking cups in the basket of the deep fryer and air fry for 5 minutes

❖ Lightly stir the mixture into each ramekin and air fry until the egg is set, another 3 to 5 minutes

43) Italian Egg Cups

Preparation Time: 5 minutes

Cooking Time: 10 minutes

Servings: 4

Nutrition: Calories 135 Fat 8g Saturated Fat 3g Cholesterol 191mg Carbs 6g Protein 10g Fiber 1g Sodium: 407mg

Ingredients:

- Olive Oil
- 1 cup marinara sauce
- 4 eggs
- 4 tablespoons shredded mozzarella cheese
- 4 teaspoons grated Parmesan cheese
- Salt
- Freshly ground black pepper
- Chopped fresh basil, for garnish

Directions:

❖ Lightly spray 4 individual ramekins with olive oil.

❖ Pour ¼ cup of marinara sauce into each ramekin.

❖ Crack one egg into each ramekin on top of the marinara sauce.

❖ Sprinkle 1 tablespoon of mozzarella and 1 tablespoon of Parmesan on top of each egg. Season it with salt and pepper.

❖ Cover each ramekin with aluminum foil. Place two of the ramekins in the fryer basket.

❖ Air fry for 5 minutes and remove the aluminum foil. Air fry until the top is lightly browned and the egg white is cooked, another 2 to 4 minutes If you prefer the yolk to be firmer, cook for 3 to 5 more minutes

❖ Repeat with the remaining two ramekins. Garnish with basil and serve.

44) Mexican Breakfast Pepper Rings

Preparation Time: 5 minutes

Cooking Time: 10 minutes

Servings: 4

Nutrition: Calories 84 Fat 5g Saturated Fat 2g Cholesterol 186mg Carbs 3g Protein 7g Fiber 1g Sodium: 83mg

Ingredients:

- Olive oil
- 1 large red, yellow, or orange bell pepper, cut into four ¾-inch rings
- 4 eggs
- Salt
- Freshly ground black pepper
- 2 teaspoons salsa

Directions:

- ❖ Lightly spray a small round air fryer–friendly pan with olive oil.
- ❖ Place 2 bell pepper rings on the pan. Crack one egg into each bell pepper ring. Season it with salt and black pepper.
- ❖ Spoon ½ teaspoon of salsa on top of each egg. Place the pan in the fryer basket. Air fry until the yolk is slightly runny, 5 to 6 minutes or until the yolk is fully cooked, 8 to 10 minutes
- ❖ Repeat with the remaining 2 pepper rings. Serve hot.
- ❖ Pair It With: Turkey sausage or turkey bacon make this a heartier morning meal.
- ❖ Air Fry Like A Pro: Use a silicone spatula to easily move the rings from the pan to your plate.

45) Cajun Breakfast Muffins

Preparation Time: 10 minutes

Cooking Time: 10 minutes

Servings: 6

Nutrition: Calories 178 Fat 9g Saturated Fat 4gCholesterol 145mg Carbs 13g Protein 11g Fiber 2g Sodium: 467mg

Ingredients:

- Olive oil
- 4 eggs, beaten
- 2¼ cups frozen hash browns, thawed
- 1 cup diced ham
- ½ cup shredded Cheddar cheese
- ½ teaspoon Cajun seasoning

Directions:

- ❖ Lightly spray 12 silicone muffin cups with olive oil.
- ❖ In a medium bowl, mix together the eggs, hash browns, ham, Cheddar cheese, and Cajun seasoning in a medium bowl.
- ❖ Spoon a heaping 1½ tablespoons of hash brown mixture into each muffin cup.
- ❖ Place the muffin cups in the fryer basket.
- ❖ Air fry until the muffins are golden brown on top and the center has set up, 8 to 10 minutes
- ❖ Make It Even Lower Calorie: Reduce or eliminate the cheese.

46) Hearty Blueberry Oatmeal

Preparation Time: 10 minutes

Cooking Time: 25 minutes

Servings: 6

Nutrition: Calories 170 Fat 3g Saturated Fat 1g Cholesterol 97mg Carbs 34g Protein 4g Fiber 4g Sodium: 97mg

Ingredients:

- 1½ cups quick oats
- 1¼ teaspoons ground cinnamon, divided
- ½ teaspoon baking powder
- Pinch salt
- 1 cup unsweetened vanilla almond milk
- ¼ cup honey
- 1 teaspoon vanilla extract
- 1 egg, beaten
- 2 cups blueberries
- Olive oil
- 1½ teaspoons sugar, divided
- 6 tablespoons low-fat whipped topping (optional)

Directions:

- ❖ In a large bowl, mix together the oats, 1 teaspoon of cinnamon, baking powder, and salt.
- ❖ In a medium bowl, whisk together the almond milk, honey, vanilla and egg.
- ❖ Pour the liquid ingredients into the oats mixture and stir to combine. Fold in the blueberries.
- ❖ Lightly spray a round air fryer–friendly pan with oil.
- ❖ Add half the blueberry mixture to the pan.
- ❖ Sprinkle ⅛ teaspoon of cinnamon and ½ teaspoon sugar over the top.
- ❖ Cover the pan with aluminum foil and place gently in the fryer basket. Air fry for 20 minutes remove the foil and air fry for an additional 5 minutes Transfer the mixture to a shallow bowl.
- ❖ Repeat with the remaining blueberry mixture, ½ teaspoon of sugar, and ⅛ teaspoon of cinnamon.
- ❖ To serve, spoon into bowls and top with whipped topping.

47) Banana Bread Pudding

Preparation Time: 10 minutes

Cooking Time: 20 minutes

Servings: 4

Nutrition: Calories 212 Fat 6g Saturated Fat 2g Carbs 38g Protein 6g Sodium: 112mg

Ingredients:

- Olive oil
- 2 medium ripe bananas, mashed
- ½ cup low-fat milk
- 2 tablespoons peanut butter
- 2 tablespoons maple syrup
- 1 teaspoon ground cinnamon
- 1 teaspoon vanilla extract
- 2 slices whole-grain bread, torn into bite-sized pieces
- ¼ cup quick oats

Directions:

- ❖ Lightly spray four individual ramekins or a deep fryer dish with olive oil.
- ❖ In a large bowl, combine the bananas, milk, peanut butter, maple syrup, cinnamon and vanilla. Using an electric mixer or whisk, mix until completely combined.
- ❖ Add the bread pieces and mix to coat the liquid mixture.
- ❖ Add the oats and mix until everything is combined.
- ❖ Transfer the mixture to the baking dish or divide it between the ramekins. Cover with aluminum foil.
- ❖ Place 2 ramekins in the basket of the deep fryer and air fry until heated through, 10 to 12 minutes
- ❖ Remove aluminum foil and bake for another 6 to 8 minutes
- ❖ Repeat with the remaining 2 ramekins. Make it even less caloric: Reduce calories by using sugar-free maple syrup or replacing peanut butter with PB2 (powdered peanut butter). Combine 4 tablespoons of peanut butter powder with 2 tablespoons of water to make 2 tablespoons of peanut butter.

48) Air fried German Pancakes

Preparation Time: 5 minutes

Cooking Time: 8 Minutes

Servings: 5

Nutrition: Calories 139 Protein 8 g Fat 4 g Carbs 18 g Fiber 3 g Sugar 1 g

Ingredients:

- Serving size: 1/2 cup batter
- 3 Full eggs
- Whole wheat flour: 1 cup
- Almond milk: 1 cup
- A pinch of salt
- Apple sauce: 2 heaping tablespoons (optional but recommended to replace the need for added oil or butter)
- For Garnishing:
- Berries
- Greek yogurt
- Confectioner sugar
- Maple syrup (optional)

Directions:

- ❖ Set the air fryer temperature to 390°F/199°C. Inside the air fryer, set the cast iron tray or ramekin as it heats. Take the blender and add all the batter ingredients to it, and combine until smooth. If the batter is too thick, simply add milk or applesauce tablespoons to smooth out. Use nonstick baking spray and spray the cast iron tray or ramekin, and then dump in a batter serving.
- ❖ Air fry the batter for 6-8 minutes
- ❖ Do not worry if top gets hard to touch. This is the advantage of using the air fryer – it provides the pancake with a good firm outer coating/edges that softens as it cools. Place the remaining batter in the refrigerator in an airtight container to freshen it up every morning.
- ❖ Garnish, and serve.

49) Air-Fried Flax Seed French toast Sticks with Berries

Preparation Time: 25 minutes

Cooking Time: 35 minutes

Servings: 4

Nutrition: Calories 361 Fat 10g Saturated Fat 1g Unsaturated Fat 7g Protein 14g Carbs 56g Fiber 10g Sugars: 30g Sodium: 218mg

Ingredients:

- Whole-grain bread: 4 slices (1 1/2-oz.)
- 2 Big Eggs
- 1/4 cup 2% reduced-fat milk
- Vanilla extract: 1 teaspoon
- Ground cinnamon: ½ teaspoon
- 1/4 cup of light brown sugar, split,
- 2/3 cup flax seed cooking spray
- 2 Cups of fresh-cut strawberries
- Maple syrup: 8 teaspoons
- Powdered sugar: 1 teaspoon

Directions:

- ❖ Cut each of the bread slices into four long sticks. In a shallow dish, whisk together eggs, milk, cinnamon, vanilla extract, and 1 tablespoon brown sugar. In a second, shallow dish, combine flaxseed meal and remaining 3 tablespoons of brown sugar.
- ❖ Dip the pieces of bread in a mixture of eggs, soak them slightly, and allow any excess to drip away. Dredge each piece in a mixture of flax seeds and coat on all sides. Cover the bits of bread with cooking oil.
- ❖ Place pieces of bread in a single layer in the air fryer basket, leave room between each piece and cook at 375 ° F in batches until golden brown and crunchy, 10 minutes, turn slices over halfway through cooking. Place 4 sticks of French toast on each plate to serve. Finish with 1/2 cup of strawberries, 2 teaspoons of maple syrup, and a powdered sugar layer. Serve right now.

50) *Breakfast Frittatas*

Preparation Time: 15 minutes

Cooking Time: 20 minutes

Servings: 2

Nutrition: Air-Fried Breakfast Bombs

Ingredients:

- Breakfast sausage: ¼ pound, completely cooked and crumbled
- Eggs: 4, lightly beaten
- Shredded cheddar cheese: ½ cup
- Red pepper: 2 tablespoons, chopped
- Green onion: 1 chopped
- Cayenne pepper: 1 pinch
- Cooking spray

Directions:

- ❖ Combine the sausage, eggs, cheddar cheese, onion, bell pepper, and cayenne in a bowl and blend. Set the temperature of the air-fryer to 360°F (180°C). Sprinkle a 6x2-inch non-stick cake pan with a cooking spray.
- ❖ Put the mixture of the eggs in the prepared cake pan. Cook in the air fryer for 18 to 20 minutes until the frittata is set.

51) *Scrambled Eggs*

Preparation Time: 4 Minutes

Cooking Time: 10 minutes

Servings: 2

Nutrition: Calories 126 kcal Fat 9g Cholesterol 200mg Carbs 1g Protein 9g Sugar: 0g

Ingredients:

- Unsalted butter: 1/3 tablespoon
- 2 Eggs
- Milk: 2 tablespoons
- Salt and black pepper to try
- Cheddar cheese: 1/8 cup

Directions:

- ❖ Place fresh butter in a fryer-safe oven/air saucepan and place it inside the fryer. Cook, about 2 minutes, at 300 degrees until fresh butter get melted.
- ❖ Whisk the milk and eggs all together then add some pepper and salt for taste. Cook for 3-4 minutes at 300 degrees, then put eggs to the inside of the fry pan and stir.
- ❖ Cook for another 2-3 minutes, then add (cheddar) cheese and stir the eggs once more. Cook another 2 minutes. Remove that pan from air fryer and instantly serve.

52) *Bacon and Eggs*

Preparation Time: 4 minutes

Cooking Time: 10 minutes

Servings: 3

Nutrition: Calories 427 Fat 29g Saturated Fat 9.3g Trans Fat 0g

Ingredients:

- 6 nitrate-free bacon strips
- Eggs: 6
- Spinach: 6 cups
- Olive oil: ½ tablespoon

Directions:

- ❖ Place the eggs on top of the second air fryer rack. Set the temperature at 270 degrees F. Air fry in hard-boiled for 15 minutes, for medium-boiled for 12 minutes and for soft boiled for 10 minutes Lift for 2 minutes and put in the ice water bath and peel shell.
- ❖ Place bacon in the lower rack. Set temperature for 12-14 minutes at 375°F and cook. 14 minutes are preferable to get extra crispy bacon. Serve with sautéed cooked spinach in olive oil.

53) *Sausage Breakfast Casserole*

Preparation Time: 10 minutes

Cooking Time: 20 minutes

Servings: 6

Nutrition: Calories 517 Fat 37g Saturated Fat 10g Trans Fat 0g Unsaturated Fat 25g Cholesterol 189mg Sodium: 1092mg Carbs 27g Fiber 3g Sugar: 4g Protein 21g

Ingredients:

- Hash browns: 1 Lb.
- Breakfast Sausage: 1 lb.
- Eggs: 4
- Green Bell Pepper: 1, diced
- Red Bell Pepper: 1, diced
- Yellow Bell Pepper: 1, diced
- Sweet onion: ¼ cup, diced

Directions:

- ❖ Cover the air fryer basket lined with foil. Put the hash browns on the bottom basket of the air fryer.
- ❖ Place the uncooked sausage over it.
- ❖ Place the peppers and the onions evenly on top.
- ❖ Cook it 10 minutes on 355°F.
- ❖ When needed, open the air fryer and mix the casserole up a bit.
- ❖ Whisk each egg in a bowl, and then pour right over the saucepan.
- ❖ Cook another 10 minutes on 355°F.
- ❖ Serve with a sprinkle of salt and pepper.

AIR FRYER
SNACK RECIPE

54) Perfect Crispy Potatoes

Preparation Time: 5 minutes

Cooking Time: 30 minutes

Servings: 4

Nutrition: Calories 365 Fat 13.2 g Carbs 48.6 gProtein 10.1 g

Ingredients:
- 1.5 pounds potatoes, halved
- 2 tbsp olive oil
- 3 garlic cloves, grated
- 1 tbsp minced fresh rosemary
- 1 tsp salt
- ¼ tsp freshly ground black pepper

Directions:
- ❖ In a bowl, mix potatoes, olive oil, garlic, rosemary, salt, and pepper, until they are well-coated. Arrange the potatoes in the air fryer and cook on 360 F for 25 minutes, shaking twice during the cooking. Cook until crispy on the outside and tender on the inside.

55) Allspice Chicken Wings

Preparation Time:

Cooking Time: 45 minutes

Servings: 8

Nutrition: Calories 332 Fat 10.1 g Carbs 31.3 gProtein 12 g

Ingredients:
- ½ tsp celery salt
- ½ tsp bay leaf powder
- ½ tsp ground black pepper
- ½ tsp paprika
- ¼ tsp dry mustard
- ¼ tsp cayenne pepper
- ¼ tsp allspice
- 2 pounds chicken wings

Directions:
- ❖ Grease the air fryer basket and preheat to 340 F. In a bowl, mix celery salt, bay leaf powder, black pepper, paprika, dry mustard, cayenne pepper, and allspice. Coat the wings thoroughly in this mixture.
- ❖ Arrange the wings in an even layer in the basket of the air fryer. Cook the chicken until it's no longer pink around the bone, for 30 minutes then, increase the temperature to 380 F and cook for 6 minutes more, until crispy on the outside.

56) Friday Night Pineapple Sticky Ribs

Preparation Time: 10 minutes

Cooking Time: 20 minutes

Servings: 4

Nutrition: Calories 316 Fat 3.1 g Carbs 1.9 gProtein 5 g

Ingredients:
- 2 lb. cut spareribs
- 7 oz salad dressing
- 1 (5-oz) can pineapple juice
- 2 cups water
- Garlic salt to taste
- Salt and black pepper

Directions:
- ❖ Sprinkle the ribs with salt and pepper, and place them in a saucepan. Pour water and cook the ribs for 12 minutes on high heat.
- ❖ Dry out the ribs and arrange them in the fryer; sprinkle with garlic salt. Cook it for 15 minutes at 390 F.
- ❖ Prepare the sauce by combining the salad dressing and the pineapple juice. Serve the ribs drizzled with the sauce.

57) Egg Roll Wrapped with Cabbage and Prawns

Preparation Time: 10 minutes

Cooking Time: 40 minutes

Servings: 4

Nutrition: Calories 215 Fat 7.9 g Carbs 6.7 gProtein 8 g

Ingredients:
- 2 tbsp vegetable oil
- 1-inch piece fresh ginger, grated
- 1 tbsp minced garlic
- 1 carrot, cut into strips
- ¼ cup chicken broth
- 2 tbsp reduced-sodium soy sauce
- 1 tbsp sugar
- 1 cup shredded Napa cabbage
- 1 tbsp sesame oil
- 8 cooked prawns, minced
- 1 egg
- 8 egg roll wrappers

Directions:
- ❖ In a skillet over high heat, heat vegetable oil, and cook ginger and garlic for 40 seconds, until fragrant. Stir in carrot and cook for another 2 minutes Pour in chicken broth, soy sauce, and sugar and bring to a boil.
- ❖ Add cabbage and let simmer until softened, for 4 minutes Remove skillet from the heat and stir in sesame oil. Let cool for 15 minutes Strain cabbage mixture, and fold in minced prawns. Whisk an egg in a small bowl. Fill each egg roll wrapper with prawn mixture, arranging the mixture just below the center of the wrapper.
- ❖ Fold the bottom part over the filling and tuck under. Fold in both sides and tightly roll up. Use the whisked egg to seal the wrapper. Repeat until all egg rolls are ready. Place the rolls into a greased air fryer basket, spray them with oil and cook for 12 minutes at 370 F, turning once halfway through.

58) Sesame Garlic Chicken Wings

Preparation Time: 10 minutes

Cooking Time: 40 minutes

Servings: 4

Nutrition: Calories 413 Fat 8.3 g Carbs 7 gProtein 8.3 g

Ingredients:

- 1-pound chicken wings
- 1 cup soy sauce, divided
- ½ cup brown sugar
- ½ cup apple cider vinegar
- 2 tbsp fresh ginger, minced
- 2 tbsp fresh garlic, minced
- 1 tsp finely ground black pepper
- 2 tbsp cornstarch
- 2 tbsp cold water
- 1 tsp sesame seeds

Directions:

- ❖ In a bowl, add chicken wings, and pour in half cup soy sauce. Refrigerate for 20 minutes; Dry out and pat dry. Arrange the wings in the air fryer and cook for 30 minutes at 380 F, turning once halfway through. Make sure you check them towards the end to avoid overcooking.
- ❖ In a skillet and over medium heat, stir sugar, half cup soy sauce, vinegar, ginger, garlic, and black pepper. Cook until sauce has reduced slightly, about 4 to 6 minutes
- ❖ Dissolve 2 tbsp of cornstarch in cold water, in a bowl, and stir in the slurry into the sauce, until it thickens, for 2 minutes Pour the sauce over wings and sprinkle with sesame seeds.

59) Savory Chicken Nuggets with Parmesan Cheese

Preparation Time: 5 minutes

Cooking Time: 20 minutes

Servings: 4

Nutrition: Calories 312 Fat 8.9 g Carbs 7 gProtein 10 g

Ingredients:

- 1 lb. chicken breast, boneless, skinless, cubed
- ½ tsp ground black pepper
- ¼ tsp kosher salt
- ¼ tsp seasoned salt
- 2 tbsp olive oil
- 5 tbsp plain breadcrumbs
- 2 tbsp panko breadcrumbs
- 2 tbsp grated Parmesan cheese

Directions:

- ❖ Preheat the air fryer to 380 F and grease. Season the chicken with pepper, kosher salt, and seasoned salt; set aside. In a bowl, pour olive oil. In a separate bowl, add crumb, and Parmesan cheese.
- ❖ Place the chicken pieces in the oil to coat, then dip into breadcrumb mixture, and transfer to the air fryer. Work in batches if needed. Lightly spray chicken with cooking spray.
- ❖ Cook the chicken for 10 minutes, flipping once halfway through. Cook until golden brown on the outside and no more pink on the inside.

60) Butternut Squash with Thyme

Preparation Time: 5 minutes

Cooking Time: 20 minutes

Servings: 4

Nutrition: Calories 219 Fat 4.3 g Carbs 9.4 gProtein 7.8 g

Ingredients:

- 2 cups peeled, butternut squash, cubed
- 1 tbsp olive oil
- ¼ tsp salt
- ¼ tsp black pepper
- ¼ tsp dried thyme
- 1 tbsp finely chopped fresh parsley

Directions:

- ❖ In a bowl, add squash, oil, salt, pepper, and thyme, and toss until squash is well-coated. Place squash in the air fryer and cook for 14 minutes at 360 F. When ready, sprinkle with freshly chopped parsley and serve chilled.

61) Chicken Breasts in Golden Crumb

Preparation Time: 10 minutes

Cooking Time: 25 minutes

Servings: 4

Nutrition: Calories 223 Fat 3.2 g Carbs 4.3 gProtein 5 g

Ingredients:

- 1 ½ lb. chicken breasts, boneless, cut into strips
- 1 egg, lightly beaten
- 1 cup seasoned breadcrumbs
- Salt and black pepper to taste
- ½ tsp dried oregano

Directions:

- ❖ Preheat the air fryer to 390 F. Season the chicken with oregano, salt, and black pepper. In a small bowl, whisk in some salt and pepper to the beaten egg. In a separate bowl, add the crumbs. Dip chicken tenders in the egg wash, then in the crumbs.
- ❖ Roll the strips in the breadcrumbs and press firmly, so the breadcrumbs stick well. Spray the chicken tenders with cooking spray and arrange them in the air fryer. Cook for 14 minutes, until no longer pink in the center, and nice and crispy on the outside.

62) Yogurt Chicken Tacos

Preparation Time: 5 minutes

Cooking Time: 20 minutes

Servings: 4

Nutrition: Calories 312 Fat 3 gCarbs 6.5 g Protein 6.2 g

Ingredients:

- 1 cup cooked chicken, shredded
- 1 cup shredded mozzarella cheese
- ¼ cup salsa
- ¼ cup Greek yogurt
- Salt and ground black pepper
- 8 flour tortillas

Directions:

- ❖ In a bowl, mix chicken, cheese, salsa, and yogurt, and season with salt and pepper. Spray one side of the tortilla with cooking spray. Lay 2 tbsp of the chicken mixture at the center of the non-oiled side of each tortilla.
- ❖ Roll tightly around the mixture. Arrange taquitos into your air fryer basket, without overcrowding. Cook in batches if needed. Place the seam side down, or it will unravel during cooking crisps.
- ❖ Cook it for 12 to 14 minutes, or until crispy, at 380 F.

63) Air Fryer Mix Party

Preparation Time: 5 minutes

Cooking Time: 20 minutes

Servings: 4

Nutrition: Calories 312 Fat 5.3 g Carbs 5 gProtein 7 g

Ingredients:

- 4 cups chopped kale leaves; stems removed
- 2 tbsp olive oil
- 1 tsp garlic powder
- ½ tsp salt
- ¼ tsp onion powder
- ¼ tsp black pepper

Directions:

- ❖ In a bowl, mix kale and oil together, until well-coated. Add in garlic, salt, onion, and pepper and toss until well-coated. Arrange half the kale leaves to air fryer, in a single layer.
- ❖ Cook for 8 minutes at 350 F, shaking once halfway through. Remove chips to a sheet to cool; do not touch.

64) Cheese Fish Balls

Preparation Time: 5 minutes

Cooking Time: 40 minutes

Servings: 6

Nutrition: Calories 234 Fat 5.2 g Carbs 4.3 gProtein 6.2 g

Ingredients:

- 1 cup smoked fish, flaked
- 2 cups cooked rice
- 2 eggs, lightly beaten
- 1 cup grated Grana Padano cheese
- ¼ cup finely chopped thyme
- Salt and black pepper to taste
- 1 cup panko crumbs

Directions:

- ❖ In a bowl, add fish, rice, eggs, Parmesan cheese, thyme, salt and pepper into a bowl; stir to combine. Shape the mixture into 12 even-sized balls. Roll the balls in the crumbs then spray with oil.
- ❖ Arrange the balls into the fryer and cook for 16 minutes at 400 F, until crispy.

65) Vermicelli Noodles & Vegetables Rolls

Preparation Time: 5 minutes

Cooking Time: 25 minutes

Servings: 8

Nutrition: Calories 312 Fat 5 g Carbs 5.4gProtein 3 g

Ingredients:

- 8 spring roll wrappers
- 1 cup cooked and cooled vermicelli noodles
- 2 garlic cloves, finely chopped
- 1 tbsp minced fresh ginger
- 2 tbsp soy sauce
- 1 tsp sesame oil
- 1 red bell pepper, seeds removed, chopped
- 1 cup finely chopped mushrooms
- 1 cup finely chopped carrot
- ½ cup finely chopped scallions

Directions:

- ❖ In a saucepan, add garlic, ginger, soy sauce, pepper, mushrooms, carrots and scallions, and sauté over high heat for a few minutes, until soft. Add vermicelli; remove from heat.
- ❖ Place spring rolls on a work surface. Distribute the balls of vegetable and noodle mixture in the center of each spring roll. Roll up spring rolls and tuck in corners and edges to create neat, secure rolls.
- ❖ Drizzle with oil and transfer to the air fryer. Cook for 12 minutes at 340 F, turning once halfway through cooking. Cook until golden brown and crispy. Serve with soy or sweet chili sauce.

66) Beef Balls with Mixed Herbs

Preparation Time: 5 minutes

Cooking Time: 25 minutes

Servings: 4

Nutrition: Calories 315 Fat 5 g Carbs 9 gProtein 8 g

Ingredients:

- 1 lb. ground beef
- 1 onion, finely chopped
- 3 garlic cloves, finely chopped
- 2 eggs
- 1 cup breadcrumbs
- ½ cup fresh mixed herbs
- 1tbsp mustard
- Salt and black pepper to taste
- Olive oil

Directions:

- ❖ In a bowl, add beef, onion, garlic, eggs, crumbs, herbs, mustard, salt, and pepper and mix with hands to combine.
- ❖ Shape into balls and arrange them in the air fryer's basket. Drizzle with oil and cook for 16 minutes at 380 F, turning once halfway through.

67) Roasted Pumpkin Seeds

Preparation Time: 10 minutes

Cooking Time: 40 minutes

Servings: 4

Nutrition: Calories 536 Fat 42.86g Calcium: 71gSodium: 571gp

Ingredients:

- 1 cup pumpkin seeds, pulp removed, rinsed
- 1 tbsp butter, melted
- 1 tbsp brown sugar
- 1 tsp orange zest
- ½ tsp cardamom
- ½ tsp salt

Directions:

- ❖ Cook the seeds for 4 minutes at 320 F, in your air fryer, to avoid moisture. In a bowl, whisk melted butter, sugar, zest, cardamom and salt.
- ❖ Add the seeds to the bowl and toss to coat thoroughly.
- ❖ Transfer the seeds to the air fryer and cook for 35 minutes at 300 F, shaking the basket every 10-12 minutes Cook until lightly browned.

68) Buttery Parmesan Broccoli Florets

Preparation Time: 5 minutes

Cooking Time: 20 minutes

Servings: 2

Nutrition: Calories 350 Fat 27 gCarbs 20gProtein 15 g

Ingredients:

- 2 tbsp butter, melted
- 1 egg white
- 1 garlic clove, grated
- ¼ tsp salt
- A pinch of black pepper
- ½ lb. broccoli florets
- ⅓ cup grated Parmesan cheese

Directions:

- ❖ In a bowl, whisk together the butter, egg, garlic, salt, and black pepper. Toss in broccoli to coat well. Top with Parmesan cheese and; toss to coat. Arrange broccoli in a single layer in the air fryer, without overcrowding. Cook it in batches for 10 minutes at 360 F. Remove to a serving plate and sprinkle with Parmesan cheese.

69) Spicy Chickpeas

Preparation Time: 5 minutes

Cooking Time: 10 minutes

Servings: 4

Nutrition: Calories 146 Fat 4.5 g Carbs 18.8 g Protein 6.3 g

Ingredients:

- 1 (15-oz.) can chickpeas rinsed and Dry-out
- 1 tablespoon olive oil
- ½ teaspoon ground cumin
- ½ teaspoon cayenne pepper
- ½ teaspoon smoked paprika
- Salt, as required

Directions:

- ❖ In a bowl, add all the ingredients and toss to coat well.
- ❖ Press "Power Button" of Air Fry Oven and turn the dial to select the "Air Fry" mode.
- ❖ Press the Time button and again turn the dial to set the cooking time to 10 minutes
- ❖ Now push the Temp button and rotate the dial to set the temperature at 390 degrees F.
- ❖ Press "Start/Pause" button to start.
- ❖ When the unit beeps to show that it is preheated, open the lid.
- ❖ Arrange the chickpeas in "Air Fry Basket" and insert in the oven.
- ❖ Serve warm.

70) *Roasted Peanuts*

Preparation Time: 5 minutes

Cooking Time: 14 minutes

Servings: 6

Nutrition: Calories 207 Fat 18 g Carbs 5.9 g Protein 9.4 g

Ingredients:
- 1½ cups raw peanuts
- Nonstick cooking spray

Directions:
- ❖ Press "Power Button" of Air Fry Oven and turn the dial to select the "Air Fry" mode. Press the Time button and again turn the dial to set the cooking time to 14 minutes
- ❖ Now push the Temp button and rotate the dial to set the temperature at 320 degrees F. Press "Start/Pause" button to start.
- ❖ When the unit beeps to show that it is preheated, open the lid.
- ❖ Arrange the peanuts in "Air Fry Basket" and insert in the oven.
- ❖ Toss the peanuts twice.
- ❖ After 9 minutes of cooking, spray the peanuts with cooking spray.
- ❖ Serve warm.

71) *Roasted Cashews*

Preparation Time: 5 minutes

Cooking Time: 5 minutes

Servings: 6

Nutrition: Calories 202 Fat 16.5 g Carbs 11.2 g Protein 5.3 g

Ingredients:
- 1½ cups raw cashew nuts
- 1 teaspoon butter, melted
- Salt and freshly ground black pepper, as needed

Directions:
- ❖ In a bowl, mix together all the ingredients.
- ❖ Press "Power Button" of Air Fry Oven and turn the dial to select the "Air Fry" mode.
- ❖ Press the Time button and again turn the dial to set the cooking time to 5 minutes
- ❖ Now push the Temp button and rotate the dial to set the temperature at 355 degrees F.
- ❖ Press "Start/Pause" button to start.
- ❖ When the unit beeps to show that it is preheated, open the lid.
- ❖ Arrange the cashews in "Air Fry Basket" and insert in the oven.
- ❖ Shake the cashews once halfway through.

72) *French Fries*

Preparation Time: 15 minutes

Cooking Time: 30 minutes

Servings: 4

Nutrition: Calories 172 Fat 10.7 g Carbs 18.6 g Protein 2.1 g

Ingredients:
- 1 lb. potatoes, peeled and cut into strips
- 3 tablespoons olive oil
- ½ teaspoon onion powder
- ½ teaspoon garlic powder
- 1 teaspoon paprika

Directions:
- ❖ In a large bowl of water, soak the potato strips for about 1 hour.
- ❖ Dry out the potato strips well and pat them dry with the paper towels.
- ❖ In a large bowl, add the potato strips and the remaining ingredients and toss to coat well.
- ❖ Press "Power Button" of Air Fry Oven and turn the dial to select the "Air Fry" mode.
- ❖ Press the Time button and again turn the dial to set the cooking time to 30 minutes
- ❖ Now push the Temp button and rotate the dial to set the temperature at 375 degrees F.
- ❖ Press "Start/Pause" button to start.
- ❖ When the unit beeps to show that it is preheated, open the lid.
- ❖ Arrange the potato fries in "Air Fry Basket" and insert in the oven.
- ❖ Serve warm.

73) Zucchini Fries

Preparation Time: 10 minutes

Cooking Time: 20 minutes

Servings: 4

Nutrition: Calories 151 Fat 8.6 g Carbs 6.9 g Protein 1.9 g

Ingredients:

- 1 lb. zucchini, sliced into 2½-inch sticks
- Salt, as required
- 2 tablespoons olive oil
- ¾ cup panko breadcrumbs

Directions:

- ❖ In a colander, add the zucchini and sprinkle with salt. Set aside for about 10 minutes. Gently pat dry the zucchini sticks with the paper towels and coat with oil.
- ❖ In a shallow dish, add the breadcrumbs. Coat the zucchini sticks with breadcrumbs evenly.
- ❖ Press "Power Button" of Air Fry Oven and turn the dial to select the "Air Fry" mode.
- ❖ Press the Time button and again turn the dial to set the cooking time to 12 minutes
- ❖ Now push the Temp button and rotate the dial to set the temperature at 400 degrees F.
- ❖ Press "Start/Pause" button to start.
- ❖ When the unit beeps to show that it is preheated, open the lid.
- ❖ Arrange the zucchini fries in "Air Fry Basket" and insert in the oven.
- ❖ Serve warm.

74) Spicy Carrot Fries

Preparation Time: 10 minutes

Cooking Time: 12 minutes

Servings: 2

Nutrition: Calories 81 Fat 8.3 g Carbs 4.7 g Protein 0.4 g

Ingredients:

- 1 large carrot, peeled and cut into sticks
- 1 tablespoon fresh rosemary, chopped finely
- 1 tablespoon olive oil
- ¼ teaspoon cayenne pepper
- Salt and ground black pepper, as required

Directions:

- ❖ In a bowl, add all ingredients and mix well. Press the "Power button" on the Air Fry oven and turn the dial to select the "Air Fry" mode.
- ❖ Press the "Time" button and turn the dial again to set the cooking time to 12 minutes
- ❖ Now press the "Temp" button and turn the dial to set the temperature to 390 degrees F.
- ❖ Press the "Start/Pause" button to begin.
- ❖ When the unit beeps to show that it is preheated, open the lid.
- ❖ Arrange the fried carrots in the "Air Fry Basket" and place in the oven.
- ❖ Serve hot.

75) Cinnamon Carrot Fries

Preparation Time: 10 minutes

Cooking Time: 12 minutes

Servings: 6

Nutrition: Calories 41 Fat 0.8 g Carbs 8.3 g Protein 0.6 g

Ingredients:

- 1 lb. carrots, peeled and cut into sticks
- 1 teaspoon maple syrup
- 1 teaspoon olive oil
- ½ teaspoon ground cinnamon
- Salt, to taste

Directions:

- ❖ In a bowl, add all the ingredients and mix well.
- ❖ Press "Power Button" of Air Fry Oven and turn the dial to select the "Air Fry" mode. Press the Time button and again turn the dial to set the cooking time to 12 minutes
- ❖ Now push the Temp button and rotate the dial to set the temperature at 400 degrees F.
- ❖ Press "Start/Pause" button to start.
- ❖ When the unit beeps to show that it is preheated, open the lid.
- ❖ Arrange the carrot fries in "Air Fry Basket" and insert in the oven.
- ❖ Serve warm.

76) Squash Fries

Preparation Time: 10 minutes

Cooking Time: 35 minutes

Servings: 2

Nutrition: Calories 134 Fat 5 g Carbs 24.3 g Protein 2.1 g

Ingredients:

- 14 oz. butternut squash, peeled, seeded and cut into strips
- 2 teaspoons olive oil
- ½ teaspoon ground cinnamon
- ½ teaspoon red chili powder
- ¼ teaspoon garlic salt
- Salt and freshly ground black pepper, as needed

Directions:

- ❖ In a bowl, add all the ingredients and toss to coat well. Press "Power Button" of Air Fry Oven and turn the dial to select the "Air Fry" mode.
- ❖ Press the Time button and again turn the dial to set the cooking time to 30 minutes. Now push the Temp button and rotate the dial to set the temperature at 400 degrees F.
- ❖ Press "Start/Pause" button to start. When the unit beeps to show that it is preheated, open the lid.
- ❖ Arrange the squash fries in "Air Fry Basket" and insert in the oven.
- ❖ Serve warm.

77) Avocado Fries

Preparation Time: 15 minutes

Cooking Time: 7 minutes

Servings: 2

Nutrition: Calories 340 Fat 14 g Carbs 30 g Protein 23 g

Ingredients:

- ¼ cup all-purpose flour
- Salt and freshly ground black pepper, as needed
- 1 egg 1 teaspoon water
- ½ cup panko breadcrumbs
- 1 avocado, peeled, pitted and sliced into 8 pieces
- Non-stick cooking spray

Directions:

- ❖ In a shallow bowl, mix together the flour, salt, and black pepper.
- ❖ In a second bowl, mix well egg and water.
- ❖ In a third bowl, put the breadcrumbs.
- ❖ Coat the avocado slices with flour mixture, then dip into egg mixture and finally, coat evenly with the breadcrumbs.
- ❖ Now, spray the avocado slices evenly with cooking spray.
- ❖ Press "Power Button" of Air Fry Oven and turn the dial to select the "Air Fry" mode.
- ❖ Press the Time button and again turn the dial to set the cooking time to 7 minutes
- ❖ Now push the Temp button and rotate the dial to set the temperature at 400 degrees F.
- ❖ Press "Start/Pause" button to start.
- ❖ When the unit beeps to show that it is preheated, open the lid.
- ❖ Arrange the avocado fries in "Air Fry Basket" and insert in the oven.
- ❖ Serve warm.

78) Dill Pickle Fries

Preparation Time: 15 minutes

Cooking Time: 15 minutes

Servings:

Nutrition: Calories 110 Fat 1.9 g Carbs 12.8 g Protein 2.7 g

Ingredients:

- 1 (16-oz.) jar spicy dill pickle spears Dry out and pat dried
- ¾ cup all-purpose flour
- ½ teaspoon paprika
- 1 egg, beaten
- ¼ cup milk
- 1 cup panko breadcrumbs
- Nonstick cooking spray

Directions:

- ❖ In a shallow dish, mix together the flour and paprika.
- ❖ In a second dish, place the milk and egg and mix well.
- ❖ In a third dish, place the breadcrumbs.
- ❖ Coat the pickles with the flour mixture, then dip them in the egg mixture and finally, coat them evenly with the breadcrumbs.
- ❖ Now, evenly spray the pickle spears with cooking spray.
- ❖ Press the "Power" button on the Air Fry oven and turn the dial to select the "Air Fry" mode.
- ❖ Press the "Time" button and turn the dial again to set the cooking time to 15 minutes
- ❖ Now press the "Temp" button and turn the dial to set the temperature to 400 degrees F.
- ❖ Press the "Start/Pause" button to begin. When the unit beeps to show that it is preheated, open the lid.
- ❖ Place the pumpkin fries in the "Air Fry Basket" and place in the oven.
- ❖ Serve hot.
- ❖ Turn the fries once halfway through cooking.
- ❖ Serve hot.

79) Mozzarella Sticks

Preparation Time: 15 minutes

Cooking Time: 12 minutes

Servings: 3

Nutrition: Calories 254 Fat 6.6 g Carbs 35.2 g Protein 12.8 g

Ingredients:

- ¼ cup white flour
- 2 eggs
- 3 tablespoons nonfat milk
- 1 cup plain breadcrumbs
- 1 lb. Mozzarella cheese block cut into 3x½-inch sticks

Directions:

- ❖ In a shallow dish, add the flour.
- ❖ In a second shallow dish, mix together the eggs, and milk.
- ❖ In a third shallow dish, place the breadcrumbs.
- ❖ Coat the Mozzarella sticks with flour, then dip into egg mixture and finally, coat evenly with the breadcrumbs.
- ❖ Press "Power Button" of Air Fry Oven and turn the dial to select the "Air Fry" mode.
- ❖ Press the Time button and again turn the dial to set the cooking time to 12 minutes
- ❖ Now push the Temp button and rotate the dial to set the temperature at 400 degrees F.
- ❖ Press "Start/Pause" button to start.
- ❖ When the unit beeps to show that it is preheated, open the lid.
- ❖ Arrange the mozzarella sticks in "Air Fry Basket" and insert in the oven.
- ❖ Serve warm

80) _Tortilla Chips_

Preparation Time: 10 minutes

Cooking Time: 3 minutes

Servings: 3

Nutrition: Calories 110 Fat 5.6 g Carbs 14.3 g Protein 1.8 g

Ingredients:

- 4 corn tortillas cut into triangles
- 1 tablespoon olive oil
- Salt, to taste

Directions:

- ❖ Coat the tortilla chips with oi and then, sprinkle each side of the tortillas with salt.
- ❖ Press "Power Button" of Air Fry Oven and turn the dial to select the "Air Fry" mode.
- ❖ Press the Time button and again turn the dial to set the cooking time to 3 minutes.
- ❖ Now push the Temp button and rotate the dial to set the temperature at 390 degrees F.
- ❖ Press "Start/Pause" button to start.
- ❖ When the unit beeps to show that it is preheated, open the lid.
- ❖ Arrange the tortilla chips in "Air Fry Basket" and insert in the oven.
- ❖ Serve warm.

81) _Apple Chips_

Preparation Time: 10 minutes

Cooking Time: 8 minutes

Servings: 2

Nutrition: Calories 83 Fat 0.2 g Carbs 22 g Protein 0.3 g

Ingredients:

- 1 apple, peeled, cored and thinly sliced
- 1 tablespoon sugar
- ½ teaspoon ground cinnamon
- Pinch of ground cardamom
- Pinch of ground ginger
- Pinch of salt

Directions:

- ❖ In a bowl, add all ingredients and stir to coat well.
- ❖ Press the "Power Button" on the Air Fry oven and turn the dial to select the "Air Fry" mode.
- ❖ Press the Time button and turn the dial again to set the cooking time to 8 minutes
- ❖ Now press the "Temp" button and turn the dial to set the temperature to 390 degrees F.
- ❖ Press the "Start/Pause" button to begin.
- ❖ When the unit beeps to show that it is preheated, open the lid.
- ❖ Arrange the apple chips in the "Air Fry Basket" and place in the oven.

82) _Kale Chips_

Preparation Time: 10 minutes

Cooking Time: 3 minutes

Servings: 4

Nutrition: Calories 115 Fat 3.5 g 0.5 g Carbs 17.9 g Protein 5.2 g

Ingredients:

- 1 head fresh kale, stems and ribs removed and cut into 1½ inch pieces
- 1 tablespoon olive oil
- 1 teaspoon soy sauce
- 1/8 teaspoon cayenne pepper
- Pinch of freshly ground black pepper

Directions:

- ❖ In a large bowl and mix together all the ingredients.
- ❖ Press "Power Button" of Air Fry Oven and turn the dial to select the "Air Fry" mode.
- ❖ Press the Time button and again turn the dial to set the cooking time to 3 minutes
- ❖ Now push the Temp button and rotate the dial to set the temperature at 390 degrees F.
- ❖ Press "Start/Pause" button to start.
- ❖ When the unit beeps to show that it is preheated, open the lid.
- ❖ Arrange the apple chips in "Air Fry Basket" and insert in the oven.
- ❖ Toss the kale chips once halfway through.

83) Beet Chips

Preparation Time: 10 minutes

Cooking Time: 15 minutes

Servings:

Nutrition: Calories 70 Fat 4.8 g Carbs 6.7 g Protein 1.1 g

Ingredients:

- 4 medium beetroots, peeled and thinly sliced
- 2 tablespoons olive oil
- ¼ teaspoon smoked paprika
- Salt, to taste

Directions:

- ❖ In a large bowl and mix together all the ingredients.
- ❖ Press "Power Button" of Air Fry Oven and turn the dial to select the "Air Fry" mode.
- ❖ Press the Time button and again turn the dial to set the cooking time to 15 minutes
- ❖ Now push the Temp button and rotate the dial to set the temperature at 325 degrees F.
- ❖ Press "Start/Pause" button to start.
- ❖ When the unit beeps to show that it is preheated, open the lid.
- ❖ Arrange the apple chips in "Air Fry Basket" and insert in the oven.
- ❖ Toss the beet chips once halfway through.
- ❖ Serve at room temperature.

84) Broccoli Salad with Goat Cheese

Preparation Time: 10 minutes

Cooking Time: 10 minutes

Servings: 4

Nutrition: Calories 380 Fat 15 g, Carbs 8 g, Protein 50g

Ingredients:

- 2 ounces broccoli florets
- 3 onions
- 3 and 1/2 ounces of goat cheese
- 4 tomatoes, sliced
- 4 bell peppers
- Cooking spray
- Salt and pepper, to taste

Directions:

- ❖ Use cooking spray to coat bell peppers, broccoli, and onions
- ❖ Preheat your air fry at 360 degrees F in "AIR FRY" mode
- ❖ Cook for 10 minutes
- ❖ Take a salad bowl and transfer the mixture into it
- ❖ Add goat cheese and tomatoes on top
- ❖ Then Season it with pepper and salt
- ❖ Serve and enjoy!

85) Fried Pumpkin Seeds

Preparation Time: 10 minutes

Cooking Time: 50 minutes

Servings: 2

Nutrition: Calories 270 Fat 21 g, Carbs 4 g, Protein 12g

Ingredients:

- 1 and 1/2 cups pumpkin seeds
- Olive oil as needed
- 1 and 1/2 teaspoons salt
- 1 teaspoon smoked paprika

Directions:

- ❖ Cut pumpkin and scrape out seeds and flesh
- ❖ Separate flesh from seeds and rinse the seeds under cold water
- ❖ Bring 2 quarter of salted water to boil and add seeds, boil for 10 minutes
- ❖ Dry out seeds and spread them on a kitchen towel
- ❖ Dry for 20 minutes
- ❖ Preheat your fryer to 350 degrees F in "AIR FRY" mode
- ❖ Take a bowl and add seeds, smoked paprika, and olive oil
- ❖ Season it with salt and transfer to your Air Fryer cooking basket
- ❖ Cook for 35 minutes, Enjoy!

86) *Potato and Paprika Roast*

Preparation Time: 35minutes

Cooking Time: 20 minutes

Servings: 4

Nutrition: Calories 540 Fat 15 g, Carbs 25g Protein 60g

Ingredients:

- 56 ounces potatoes, peeled and cubed
- 2 tablespoons spicy paprika
- 4 cups Greek yogurt
- 4 tablespoons olive oil, divided
- Salt and pepper, to taste

Directions:

- ❖ Preheat air fryer to 360 degrees F in "AIR FRY" mode.
- ❖ Soak potatoes in water. Allow to soak for 30 minutes. Take a paper towel then pat dry and pat dry.
- ❖ Add paprika, salt, pepper and half of the oil to a bowl.
- ❖ Mix them together well. Coat the potatoes in the mixture. Bake in the air fryer for 20 minutes.
- ❖ Meanwhile, mix remaining oil and yogurt
- ❖ Season with salt and pepper
- ❖ Serve with the yogurt and enjoy!

87) *Banana Fritters*

Preparation Time: 10 minutes

Cooking Time: 16 minutes

Servings: 6

Nutrition: Calories 240 Fat 10 g Carbs 30 g Protein 5 g

Ingredients:

- 1 medium butternut squash
- 2 teaspoons cumin seeds
- 1 large pinch chili flakes
- 1 tablespoon olive oil
- 1 and 1/2-ounces pine nuts
- 1 small bunch fresh coriander, chopped

Directions:

- ❖ Preheat your Air Fryer to 340 degrees F in "AIR FRY" mode
- ❖ Take a bowl and add salt, sesame seeds, water and mix them well until a nice batter form
- ❖ Coat the bananas with the flour mixture and transfer them to the fryer basket
- ❖ Cook for 8 minutes
- ❖ Enjoy!

88) *Onion Pakora*

Preparation Time: 10 minutes

Cooking Time: 10 minutes

Servings: 4

Nutrition: Calories 280 Fat 20 g, Carbs 28g Protein 8g

Ingredients:

- 1 cup Gram Flour
- 1/4 cup almond flour
- 2 teaspoons olive oil
- 4 whole onions
- 2 green chili
- 1 tablespoon coriander
- 1/4 teaspoon carom
- 1/8 teaspoon chili powder
- Salt as needed

Directions:

- ❖ Slice your onion into individual slices
- ❖ Chop the green chilies
- ❖ Cut up the coriander into equal-sized portions
- ❖ Take a bowl and add carom, turmeric powder, salt, and chili powder
- ❖ Add onion, chilies, and coriander
- ❖ Mix well
- ❖ Add water and keep mixing until you have a dough-like consistency
- ❖ Mix the dough and form balls
- ❖ Pre-heat your Fryer to 392 degrees Fahrenheit in "AIR FRY" mode
- ❖ Cook for 8 minutes
- ❖ Make sure to keep checking after every 6 minutes to ensure that they are not burnt

AIR FRYER
LUNCH RECIPE

89) Juicy Pork Chops

Preparation Time: 10 minutes

Cooking Time: 16 minutes

Servings: 4

Nutrition: Calories 279Fat 22.3 g Carbs 0.6 g Protein 18.1 g

Ingredients:

- 4 pork chops, boneless
- 2 tsp olive oil
- ½ tsp celery seed
- ½ tsp parsley
- ½ tsp granulated onion
- ½ tsp granulated garlic
- ¼ tsp sugar
- ½ tsp salt

Directions:

- ❖ In a small bowl, mix together oil, celery seed, parsley, granulated onion, granulated garlic, sugar, and salt.
- ❖ Rub seasoning mixture all over the pork chops.
- ❖ Place pork chops on the air fryer oven pan and cook at 350 F for 8 minutes
- ❖ Turn pork chops to other side and cook for 8 minutes more.
- ❖ Serve and enjoy.

90) Crispy Meatballs

Preparation Time: 10 minutes

Cooking Time: 12 minutes

Servings: 8

Nutrition: Calories 263Fat 9 g Carbs 7.5 g Protein 35.9 g

Ingredients:

- 1 lb. ground pork
- 1 lb. ground beef
- 1 tbsp Worcestershire sauce
- ½ cup feta cheese, crumbled
- ½ cup breadcrumbs
- 2 eggs, lightly beaten
- ¼ cup fresh parsley, chopped
- 1 tbsp garlic, minced
- 1 onion, chopped
- ¼ tsp pepper
- 1 tsp salt

Directions:

- ❖ Add all ingredients to mixing bowl and mix until well combined.
- ❖ Spray the air fryer pan with cooking spray.
- ❖ Make small balls from the meat mixture and place on a frying pan and air fry t 400 F for 10-12 minutes
- ❖ Serve and enjoy.

91) Flavorful Steak

Preparation Time: 10 minutes

Cooking Time: 18 minutes

Servings: 2

Nutrition: Calories 361 Fat 10.9 g Carbs 0.5 g Protein 61.6 g

Ingredients:

- 2 steaks, rinsed and pat dry
- ½ tsp garlic powder
- 1 tsp olive oil
- Pepper
- Salt

Directions:

- ❖ Rub steaks with olive oil and season with garlic powder, pepper, and salt.
- ❖ Preheat the instant vortex air fryer oven to 400 F.
- ❖ Place steaks on air fryer oven pan and air fry for 10-18 minutes turn halfway through.
- ❖ Serve and enjoy.

92) Lemon Garlic Lamb Chops

Preparation Time: 10 minutes

Cooking Time: 6 minutes

Servings: 6

Nutrition: Calories 69 Fat 6 g Carbs 1.2 g Protein 3 g

Ingredients:

- Add lamb chops in a mixing bowl. Add remaining ingredients on top of lamb chops and coat well.
- Arrange lamb chops on air fryer oven tray and air fry at 400 F for 3 minutes. Turn lamb chops to another side and air fry for 3 minutes more.
- Serve and enjoy.

Directions:

- ❖ Add lamb chops in a mixing bowl. Add remaining ingredients on top of lamb chops and coat well.
- ❖ Arrange lamb chops on air fryer oven tray and air fry at 400 F for 3 minutes. Turn lamb chops to another side and air fry for 3 minutes more.
- ❖ Serve and enjoy.

93) Honey Mustard Pork Tenderloin

Preparation Time: 10 minutes

Cooking Time: 26 minutes

Servings: 4

Nutrition: Calories 195 Fat 4.1 g Carbs 8 g Protein 30.5 g

Ingredients:

- 1 lb. pork tenderloin
- 1 tsp sriracha sauce
- 1 tbsp garlic, minced
- 2 tbsp soy sauce
- 1 ½ tbsp honey
- ¾ tbsp Dijon mustard
- 1 tbsp mustard

Directions:

- ❖ Add sriracha sauce, garlic, soy sauce, honey, Dijon mustard, and mustard into the large zip-lock bag and mix well.
- ❖ Add pork tenderloin into the bag. Seal bag and place in the refrigerator for overnight. Preheat the instant vortex air fryer oven to 380 F.Spray instant vortex air fryer tray with cooking spray then place marinated pork tenderloin on a tray and air fry for 26 minutes Turn pork tenderloin after every 5 minutes. Slice and serve.

94) Easy Rosemary Lamb Chops

Preparation Time: 10 minutes

Cooking Time: 6 minutes

Servings: 4

Nutrition: Calories 267 Fat 21.7 g Carbs 1.4 g Protein 16.9 g

Ingredients:

- 4 lamb chops
- 2 tbsp dried rosemary
- ¼ cup fresh lemon juice
- Pepper
- Salt

Directions:

- ❖ In a small bowl, mix together lemon juice, rosemary, pepper, and salt. Brush lemon juice rosemary mixture over lamb chops.
- ❖ Place lamb chops on air fryer oven tray and air fry at 400 F for 3 minutes. Turn lamb chops to the other side and cook for 3 minutes more. Serve and enjoy.

95) BBQ Pork Ribs

Preparation Time: 10 minutes

Cooking Time: 12 minutes

Servings: 6

Nutrition: Calories 145 Fat 7 g Carbs 10 g Protein 9 g

Ingredients:

- 1 slab baby back pork ribs, cut into pieces
- ½ cup BBQ sauce
- ½ tsp paprika
- Salt

Directions:

- ❖ Add pork ribs in a mixing bowl. Add BBQ sauce, paprika, and salt over pork ribs and coat well and set aside for 30 minutes
- ❖ Preheat the instant vortex air fryer oven to 350 F. Arrange marinated pork ribs on instant vortex air fryer oven pan and cook for 10-12 minutes Turn halfway through.
- ❖ Serve and enjoy.

96) Juicy Steak Bites

Preparation Time: 10 minutes

Cooking Time: 9 minutes

Servings: 4

Nutrition: Calories 241 Fat 10.6 g Carbs 0 g Protein 34.4 g

Ingredients:

- 1 lb. sirloin steak, cut into bite-size pieces
- 1 tbsp steak seasoning
- 1 tbsp olive oil
- Pepper
- Salt

Directions:

- ❖ Preheat the instant vortex air fryer oven to 390 F.
- ❖ Add steak pieces into the large mixing bowl. Add steak seasoning, oil, pepper, and salt over steak pieces and toss until well coated.
- ❖ Transfer steak pieces on instant vortex air fryer pan and air fry for 5 minutes
- ❖ Turn steak pieces to the other side and cook for 4 minutes more.
- ❖ Serve and enjoy.

97) Greek Lamb Chops

Preparation Time: 10 minutes

Cooking Time: 10 minutes

Servings: 4

Nutrition: Calories 538 Fat 29.4 g Carbs 1.3 g Protein 64 g

Ingredients:

- 2 lbs. lamb chops
- 2 tsp garlic, minced
- 1 ½ tsp dried oregano
- ¼ cup fresh lemon juice
- ¼ cup olive oil
- ½ tsp pepper
- 1 tsp salt

Directions:

- ❖ Add lamb chops in a mixing bowl. Add remaining ingredients over the lamb chops and coat well.
- ❖ Arrange lamb chops on the air fryer oven tray and cook at 400 F for 5 minutes
- ❖ Turn lamb chops and cook for 5 minutes more.
- ❖ Serve and enjoy.

98) Easy Beef Roast

Preparation Time: 10 minutes

Cooking Time: 45 minutes

Servings: 6

Nutrition: Calories 365 Fat 13.2 g Carbs 0.5 g Protein 57.4 g

Ingredients:

- 2 ½ lbs. beef roast
- 2 tbsp Italian seasoning

Directions:

- ❖ Arrange roast on the rotisserie spite.
- ❖ Rub roast with Italian seasoning then insert into the instant vortex air fryer oven.
- ❖ Air fry at 350 F for 45 minutes or until the internal temperature of the roast reaches to 145 F.
- ❖ Slice and serve.

99) Herb Butter Rib-eye Steak

Preparation Time: 10 minutes

Cooking Time: 14 minutes

Servings: 4

Nutrition: Calories 416 Fat 36.7 g Carbs 0.7 g Protein 20.3 g

Ingredients:
- INGREDIENTS:
- 2 lbs. rib eye steak, bone-in
- 1 tsp fresh rosemary, chopped
- 1 tsp fresh thyme, chopped
- 1 tsp fresh chives, chopped
- 2 tsp fresh parsley, chopped
- 1 tsp garlic, minced
- ¼ cup butter softened
- Pepper
- Salt

Directions:
- ❖ In a small bowl, combine together butter and herbs.
- ❖ Rub herb butter on rib-eye steak and place it in the refrigerator for 30 minutes
- ❖ Place marinated steak on instant vortex air fryer oven pan and cook at 400 F for 12-14 minutes
- ❖ Serve and enjoy.

100) Classic Beef Jerky

Preparation Time: 10 minutes

Cooking Time: 4 hours

Servings: 4

Nutrition: Calories 133 Fat 4.7 g Carbs 9.4 g Protein 13.4 g

Ingredients:
- 2 lbs. London broil, sliced thinly
- 1 tsp onion powder
- 3 tbsp brown sugar
- 3 tbsp soy sauce
- 1 tsp olive oil
- 3/4 tsp garlic powder

Directions:
- ❖ Add all ingredients except meat in the large zip-lock bag.
- ❖ Mix until well combined. Add meat in the bag.
- ❖ Seal bag and massage gently to cover the meat with marinade.
- ❖ Let marinate the meat for 1 hour.
- ❖ Arrange marinated meat slices on instant vortex air fryer tray and dehydrate at 160 F for 4 hours.

101) BBQ Pork Chops

Preparation Time: 10 minutes

Cooking Time: 7 minutes

Servings: 4

Nutrition: Calories 273 Fat 20.2 g Carbs 3.4 g Protein 18.4 g

Ingredients:
- 4 pork chops
- For rub:
- ½ tsp allspice
- ½ tsp dry mustard
- 1 tsp ground cumin
- 1 tsp garlic powder
- ½ tsp chili powder
- ½ tsp paprika
- 1 tbsp brown sugar
- 1 tsp salt

Directions:
- ❖ In a small bowl, mix together all rub ingredients and rub all over pork chops.
- ❖ Arrange pork chops on air fryer tray and air fry at 400 F for 5.
- ❖ Turn pork chops to other side and air fry for 2 minutes more.
- ❖ Serve and enjoy.

102) Simple Beef Patties

Preparation Time: 10 minutes

Cooking Time: 13 minutes

Servings: 4

Nutrition: Calories 212 Fat 7.1 g Carbs 0.4 g Protein 34.5 g

Ingredients:
- 1 lb. ground beef
- ½ tsp garlic powder
- ¼ tsp onion powder
- Pepper
- Salt

Directions:
- ❖ Preheat the instant vortex air fryer oven to 400 F.
- ❖ Add ground meat, garlic powder, onion powder, pepper, and salt into the mixing bowl and mix until well combined.
- ❖ Make even shape patties from meat mixture and arrange on air fryer pan.
- ❖ Place pan in instant vortex air fryer oven.
- ❖ Cook patties for 10 minutes Turn patties after 5 minutes
- ❖ Serve and enjoy.

103) _Marinated Pork Chops_

Preparation Time: 10 minutes

Cooking Time: 30 minutes

Servings: 2

Nutrition: Calories 424 Fat 21.3 g Carbs 30.8 g Protein 25.5 g

Ingredients:

- 2 pork chops, boneless
- 1 tsp garlic powder
- ½ cup flour
- 1 cup buttermilk
- Pepper
- Salt

Directions:

- ❖ Add pork chops and buttermilk in a zip-lock bag. Seal bag and place in the refrigerator for overnight.
- ❖ In another zip-lock bag add flour, garlic powder, pepper, and salt.
- ❖ Remove marinated pork chops from buttermilk and add in flour mixture and shake until well coated.
- ❖ Preheat the instant vortex air fryer oven to 380 F.
- ❖ Spray air fryer tray with cooking spray.
- ❖ Arrange pork chops on a tray and air fryer for 28-30 minutes Turn pork chops after 18 minutes
- ❖ Serve and enjoy.

104) _Simple Beef Sirloin Roast_

Preparation Time: 10 minutes

Cooking Time: 50 minutes

Servings: 8

Nutrition:

Ingredients:

- 2½ pounds sirloin roast
- Salt and ground black pepper, as required

Directions:

- ❖ Generously rub the roast with salt and black pepper.
- ❖ Insert the rotisserie rod through the roast.
- ❖ Insert rotisserie forks, one on each side of the rod to secure the rod to the broiler.
- ❖ Place the drip pan on the bottom of the oven cooking chamber of the Instant Vortex Plus air fryer.
- ❖ Select "Roast" and then set the temperature to 350 degrees F.
- ❖ Set the timer for 50 minutes and press the "Start" button.
- ❖ When the display shows "Add Food" press the red lever down and load the left side of the rod into the Vortex.
- ❖ Now, slide the left side of the rod into the groove along the metal bar so that it does not move. Then, close the door and tap "Rotate." Press the red lever to release the rod when the cooking time is over.
- ❖ Remove from the Vortex and place the roast on a plate for about 10 minutes before slicing. Using a sharp knife, cut the roast into desired size slices and serve..

105) _Seasoned Beef Roast_

Preparation Time: 10 minutes

Cooking Time: 45 minutes

Servings: 10

Nutrition: Calories 269 Fat 9.9 g Carbs 0 gFiber 0 g

Ingredients:

- 3 pounds beef top roast
- 1 tablespoon olive oil
- 2 tablespoons Montreal steak seasoning

Directions:

- ❖ Coat the roast with oil and then rub with the seasoning generously.
- ❖ With kitchen twines, tie the roast to keep it compact. Arrange the roast onto the cooking tray.
- ❖ Arrange the drip pan in the bottom of Instant Vortex plus Air Fryer Oven cooking chamber.
- ❖ Select "Air Fry" and then adjust the temperature to 360 degrees F. Set the timer for 45 minutes and press the "Start".
- ❖ When the display shows "Add Food" insert the cooking tray in the center position.
- ❖ When the display shows "Turn Food" do nothing.
- ❖ When cooking time is complete, remove the tray from Vortex and place the roast onto a platter for about 10 minutes before slicing. With a sharp knife, cut the roast into desired sized slices and serve.

106) *Bacon Wrapped Filet Mignon*

Preparation Time: 10 minutes

Cooking Time:

Servings: 2

Nutrition:

Ingredients:

- 2 bacon slices
- 2 (4-ounce) filet mignon
- Salt and ground black pepper, as required
- Olive oil cooking spray

Directions:

- ❖ Wrap 1 bacon slice around each filet mignon and secure with toothpicks.
- ❖ Season the filets with the salt and black pepper lightly.
- ❖ Arrange the filet mignon onto a coking rack and spray with cooking spray.
- ❖ Arrange the drip pan in the bottom of Instant Vortex plus Air Fryer Oven cooking chamber.
- ❖ Select "Air Fry" and then adjust the temperature to 375 degrees F.
- ❖ Set the timer for 15 minutes and press the "Start".
- ❖ When the display shows "Add Food" insert the cooking rack in the center position.
- ❖ When the display shows "Turn Food" turn the filets.
- ❖ When cooking time is complete, remove the rack from Vortex and serve hot.

107) *Beef Burgers*

Preparation Time: 15 minutes

Cooking Time: 18 minutes

Servings: 4

Nutrition: Calories 402 Fat 18 g Carbs 6.3 gProtein 44.4 g

Ingredients:

- For Burgers:
- 1-pound ground beef
- ½ cup panko breadcrumbs
- ¼ cup onion, chopped finely
- 3 tablespoons Dijon mustard
- 3 teaspoons low-sodium soy sauce
- 2 teaspoons fresh rosemary, chopped finely
- Salt, to taste
- For Topping:
- 2 tablespoons Dijon mustard
- 1 tablespoon brown sugar
- 1 teaspoon soy sauce
- 4 Gruyere cheese slices

Directions:

- ❖ In a large bowl, add all ingredients and mix until well combined.
- ❖ Form 4 equal-sized meatballs from the mixture.
- ❖ Arrange the patties on a baking tray.
- ❖ Place the cooking tray on the bottom of the cooking chamber of the Instant Vortex Plus Air Fryer oven.
- ❖ Select "Air Fry" and then set the temperature to 370 degrees F.
- ❖ Set the timer for 15 minutes and press the "Start" button.
- ❖ When the display shows "Add Food" insert the cooking rack in the center position.
- ❖ When the display shows "Turn Food" flip the burgers.
- ❖ Meanwhile, for the sauce: in a small bowl, add the mustard, brown sugar and soy sauce and mix well.
- ❖ When the cooking time is complete, remove the tray from the Vortex and coat the burgers with the sauce.
- ❖ Top each burger with 1 slice of cheese.
- ❖ Return the tray to the cooking chamber and select "Broil".
- ❖ Set the timer for 3 minutes and press "Start".
- ❖ When the cooking time is complete, remove the tray from the Vortex and serve hot.

108) *Season and Salt-Cured Beef*

Preparation Time: 15 minutes

Cooking Time: 3 hours

Servings: 4

Nutrition: Calories 372 Fat 10.7 g Carbs 12 gProtein 53.8 g

Ingredients:

- 1½ pounds beef round, trimmed
- ½ cup Worcestershire sauce
- ½ cup low-sodium soy sauce
- 2 teaspoons honey
- 1 teaspoon liquid smoke
- 2 teaspoons onion powder
- ½ teaspoon red pepper flakes
- Ground black pepper, as required

Directions:

- In a zip-top bag, place the beef and freeze for 1-2 hours to firm up.
- Place the meat onto a cutting board and cut against the grain into 1/8-¼-inch strips.
- In a large bowl, add the remaining ingredients and mix until well combined.
- Add the steak slices and coat with the mixture generously.
- Refrigerate to marinate for about 4-6 hours.
- Remove the beef slices from bowl and with paper towels, pat dry them.
- Divide the steak strips onto the cooking trays and arrange in an even layer.
- Select "Dehydrate" and then adjust the temperature to 160 degrees F.
- Set the timer for 3 hours and press the "Start".
- When the display shows "Add Food" insert 1 tray in the top position and another in the center position.
- After 1½ hours, switch the position of cooking trays.
- Meanwhile, in a small pan, add the remaining ingredients over medium heat and cook for about 10 minutes, stirring occasionally.
- When cooking time is complete, remove the trays from Vortex.

109) *Sweet & Spicy Meatballs*

Preparation Time: 20 minutes

Cooking Time: 30 minutes

Servings: 8

Nutrition: Calories 411 Fat 11.1 g Carbs 38.8 gProtein 38.9 g

Ingredients:

- For Meatballs:
- 2 pounds lean ground beef
- 2/3 cup quick-cooking oats
- ½ cup Ritz crackers, crushed
- 1 (5-ounce) can evaporated milk
- 2 large eggs, beaten lightly
- 1 teaspoon honey
- 1 tablespoon dried onion, minced
- 1 teaspoon garlic powder
- 1 teaspoon ground cumin
- Salt and ground black pepper, as required
- For Sauce:
- 1/3 cup orange marmalade
- 1/3 cup honey
- 1/3 cup brown sugar
- 2 tablespoons cornstarch
- 2 tablespoons soy sauce
- 1-2 tablespoons hot sauce
- 1 tablespoon Worcestershire sauce

Directions:

- For meatballs: in a large bowl, add all the ingredients and mix until well combined.
- Make 1½-inch balls from the mixture.
- Arrange half of the meatballs onto a cooking tray in a single layer.
- Arrange the drip pan in the bottom of Instant Vortex Plus Air Fryer Oven cooking chamber.
- Select "Air Fry" and then adjust the temperature to 380 degrees F.
- Set the timer for 15 minutes and press the "Start".
- When the display shows "Add Food" insert the cooking tray in the center position.
- When the display shows "Turn Food" turn the meatballs.
- When cooking time is complete, remove the tray from Vortex.
- Repeat with the remaining meatballs.
- Meanwhile, for sauce: in a small pan, add all the ingredients over medium heat and cook until thickened, stirring continuously.
- Serve the meatballs with the topping of sauce.

110) *Spiced Pork Shoulder*

Preparation Time: 15 minutes

Cooking Time: 55 minutes

Servings: 6

Nutrition: Calories 445 Fat 32.5 g Carbs 0.7 gProtein 35.4 g

Ingredients:

- 1 teaspoon ground cumin
- 1 teaspoon cayenne pepper
- 1 teaspoon garlic powder
- Salt and ground black pepper, as required
- 2 pounds skin-on pork shoulder

Directions:

- ❖ In a small bowl, mix together the spices, salt and black pepper.
- ❖ Arrange the pork shoulder on a cutting board, skin side down.
- ❖ Season the inside of the pork shoulder with salt and black pepper.
- ❖ Using kitchen twine, tie the pork shoulder into a long round cylinder.
- ❖ Season the outside of the pork shoulder with the spice mixture.
- ❖ Insert the rotisserie rod through the pork shoulder.
- ❖ Insert rotisserie forks, one on each side of the rod to secure the pork shoulder.
- ❖ Place the drip pan on the bottom of the Instant Vortex Plus Air Fryer oven cooking chamber.
- ❖ Select "Roast" and then set the temperature to 350 degrees F.
- ❖ Set the timer for 55 minutes and press the "Start" button.
- ❖ When the display shows "Add Food" press the red lever down and load the left side of the rod into the Vortex.
- ❖ Now, slide the left side of the rod into the groove along the metal bar so that it does not move.
- ❖ Then, close the door and tap "Rotate."
- ❖ Press the red lever to release the rod when the cooking time is over.
- ❖ Remove the pork from the Vortex and place it on a plate for about 10 minutes before slicing.
- ❖ Using a sharp knife, cut pork shoulder into desired size slices and serve.

111) *Seasoned Pork Tenderloin*

Preparation Time: 10 minutes

Cooking Time: 45 minutes

Servings: 5

Nutrition: Calories 195 Fat 4.8 g Carbs 0 gProtein 35.6 g

Ingredients:

- 1½ pounds pork tenderloin
- 2-3 tablespoons BBQ pork seasoning

Directions:

- ❖ Rub the pork with seasoning generously. Insert the rotisserie rod through the pork tenderloin.
- ❖ Insert the rotisserie forks, one on each side of the rod to secure the pork tenderloin.
- ❖ Arrange the drip pan in the bottom of Instant Vortex plus Air Fryer Oven cooking chamber.
- ❖ Select "Roast" and then adjust the temperature to 360 degrees F.
- ❖ Set the timer for 45 minutes and press the "Start".
- ❖ When the display shows "Add Food" press the red lever down and load the left side of the rod into the Vortex.
- ❖ Now, slide the rod's left side into the groove along the metal bar so it doesn't move.
- ❖ Then, close the door and touch "Rotate".
- ❖ Press the red lever to release the rod when cooking time is complete.
- ❖ Remove the pork from Vortex and place onto a platter for about 10 minutes before slicing.
- ❖ With a sharp knife, cut the roast into desired sized slices and serve.

112) Garlicky Pork Tenderloin

Preparation Time: 15 minutes

Cooking Time: 20 minutes

Servings: 5

Nutrition: Calories 202 Fat 4.8 g Carbs 1.7 gProtein 35.9 g

Ingredients:

- 1½ pounds pork tenderloin
- Nonstick cooking spray
- 2 small heads roasted garlic
- Salt and ground black pepper, as required

Directions:

- ❖ Lightly, spray all the sides of pork with cooking spray and then, season with salt and black pepper.
- ❖ Now, rub the pork with roasted garlic. Arrange the roast onto the lightly greased cooking tray.
- ❖ Arrange the drip pan in the bottom of Instant Vortex plus Air Fryer Oven cooking chamber.
- ❖ Select "Air Fry" and then adjust the temperature to 400 degrees F. Set the timer for 20 minutes and press the "Start".
- ❖ When the display shows "Add Food" insert the cooking tray in the center position.
- ❖ When the display shows "Turn Food" turn the pork.
- ❖ When cooking time is complete, remove the tray from Vortex and place the roast onto a platter for about 10 minutes before slicing. With a sharp knife, cut the roast into desired sized slices and serve.

113) Glazed Pork Tenderloin

Preparation Time: 15 minutes

Cooking Time: 20 minutes

Servings: 3

Nutrition: Calories 269 Fat 5.3 g Carbs 13.5 gProtein 39.7 g

Ingredients:

- 1-pound pork tenderloin
- 2 tablespoons Sriracha
- 2 tablespoons honey
- Salt, as required

Directions:

- ❖ Insert the rotisserie rod through the pork tenderloin.
- ❖ Insert rotisserie forks, one on each side of the rod to secure the pork tenderloin.
- ❖ In a small bowl, add the Sriracha, honey and salt and mix well.
- ❖ Brush the pork tenderloin evenly with the honey mixture.
- ❖ Place the drip pan on the bottom of the Instant Vortex Plus Air Fryer oven cooking chamber.
- ❖ Select "Air Fry" and then set the temperature to 350 degrees F.
- ❖ Set the timer for 20 minutes and press the "Start" button.
- ❖ When the display shows "Add Food" press the red lever down and load the left side of the rod into the Vortex.
- ❖ Now, slide the left side of the rod into the groove along the metal bar so it doesn't move.
- ❖ Then, close the door and tap "Rotate."
- ❖ Press the red lever to release the rod when the cooking time is over.
- ❖ Remove the pork from the Vortex and place it on a plate for about 10 minutes before slicing.
- ❖ Using a sharp knife, cut the roast into desired size slices and serve.

114)   *Country Style Pork Tenderloin*

Preparation Time: 15 minutes

Cooking Time: 25 minutes

Servings: 3

Nutrition: Calories 277 Fat 5.7 g Carbs 14.2 gProtein 40.7 g

Ingredients:

- 1-pound pork tenderloin
- 1 tablespoon garlic, minced
- 2 tablespoons soy sauce
- 2 tablespoons honey
- 1 tablespoon Dijon mustard
- 1 tablespoon grain mustard
- 1 teaspoon Sriracha sauce

Directions:

- ❖ In a large bowl, add all ingredients except the pork and mix well.
- ❖ Add the pork tenderloin and coat generously with the mixture.
- ❖ Place in the refrigerator to marinate for 2-3 hours.
- ❖ Remove the pork tenderloin from the bowl, reserving the marinade.
- ❖ Place the pork tenderloin on the lightly greased cooking tray.
- ❖ Place the drip pan on the bottom of the cooking chamber of the Instant Vortex Plus Air Fryer oven.
- ❖ Select "Air Fry" and then set the temperature to 380 degrees F.
- ❖ Set the timer for 25 minutes and press the "Start" button.
- ❖ When the display shows "Add Food" insert the cooking tray in the center position.
- ❖ When the display shows "Turn Food" turn the pork and oats with the reserved marinade.
- ❖ When the cooking time is complete, remove the tray from the Vortex and place the pork tenderloin on a serving platter for about 10 minutes before slicing.
- ❖ Using a sharp knife, cut the pork tenderloin into desired size slices and serve.

115)   *Seasoned Pork Chops*

Preparation Time: 10 minutes

Cooking Time: 12 minutes

Servings: 4

Nutrition: Calories 285 Fat 9.5 g Carbs 1.5 gProtein 44.5 g

Ingredients:

- 4 (6-ounce) boneless pork chops
- 2 tablespoons pork rub
- 1 tablespoon olive oil

Directions:

- ❖ Coat both sides of the pork chops with the oil and then, rub with the pork rub.
- ❖ Place the pork chops onto the lightly greased cooking tray.
- ❖ Arrange the drip pan in the bottom of Instant Vortex Plus Air Fryer Oven cooking chamber.
- ❖ Select "Air Fry" and then adjust the temperature to 400 degrees F.
- ❖ Set the timer for 12 minutes and press the "Start".
- ❖ When the display shows "Add Food" insert the cooking tray in the center position.
- ❖ When the display shows "Turn Food" turn the pork chops.
- ❖ When cooking time is complete, remove the tray from Vortex and serve hot.

116) Breaded Pork Chops

Preparation Time: 15 minutes

Cooking Time: 28 minutes

Servings: 2

Nutrition: Calories 370 Fat 6.4 g Carbs 30.7 gProtein 44.6 g

Ingredients:

- 2 (5-ounce) boneless pork chops
- 1 cup buttermilk
- ½ cup flour
- 1 teaspoon garlic powder
- Salt and ground black pepper, as required
- Olive oil cooking spray

Directions:

- ❖ In a bowl, place the chops and buttermilk and refrigerate, covered for about 12 hours.
- ❖ Remove the chops from the bowl of buttermilk, discarding the buttermilk.
- ❖ In a shallow dish, mix together the flour, garlic powder, salt, and black pepper.
- ❖ Coat the chops with flour mixture generously.
- ❖ Place the pork chops onto the cooking tray and spray with the cooking spray.
- ❖ Arrange the drip pan in the bottom of Instant Vortex Plus Air Fryer Oven cooking chamber.
- ❖ Select "Air Fry" and then adjust the temperature to 380 degrees F.
- ❖ Set the timer for 28 minutes and press the "Start".
- ❖ When the display shows "Add Food" insert the cooking tray in the center position.
- ❖ When the display shows "Turn Food" turn the pork chops.
- ❖ When cooking time is complete, remove the tray from Vortex and serve hot.

117) Lamb Burgers

Preparation Time: 15 minutes

Cooking Time: 8 minutes

Servings: 6

Nutrition: Calories 285 Fat 11.1 g Carbs 0.9 gProtein 42.6 g

Ingredients:

- 2 pounds ground lamb
- 1 tablespoon onion powder
- Salt and ground black pepper, as required

Directions:

- ❖ In a bowl, add all the ingredients and mix well.
- ❖ Make 6 equal-sized patties from the mixture.
- ❖ Arrange the patties onto a cooking tray.
- ❖ Arrange the drip pan in the bottom of Instant Vortex Plus Air Fryer Oven cooking chamber.
- ❖ Select "Air Fry" and then adjust the temperature to 360 degrees F.
- ❖ Set the timer for 8 minutes and press the "Start".
- ❖ When the display shows "Add Food" insert the cooking rack in the center position.
- ❖ When the display shows "Turn Food" turn the burgers.
- ❖ When cooking time is complete, remove the tray from Vortex and serve hot.

118) Salmon

Preparation Time: 5 minutes

Cooking Time: 12 minutes

Servings: 2

Nutrition: Calories 288 CalCarbs 1.4g Fat 18.9g Protein 28.3g

Ingredients:

- 2 salmon fillets, wild-caught, each about 1 ½ inch thick
- 1 teaspoon ground black pepper
- 2 teaspoons paprika
- 1 teaspoon salt
- 2 teaspoons olive oil

Directions:

- ❖ Switch on the air fryer, insert fryer basket, grease it with olive oil, then shut with its lid, set the fryer at 390 degrees F and preheat for 5 minutes. Meanwhile, rub each salmon fillet with oil and then season with black pepper, paprika, and salt.
- ❖ Open the fryer, add seasoned salmon in it, close with its lid and cook for 7 minutes until nicely golden and cooked, flipping the fillets halfway through the frying.
- ❖ When air fryer beeps, open its lid, transfer salmon onto a serving plate and serve.

119) Parmesan Shrimp

Preparation Time: 10 minutes

Cooking Time: 10 minutes

Servings: 6

Nutrition: Calories 307 CalCarbs 12g Fat 16.4g Protein 27.6g

Ingredients:

- 2 pounds jumbo shrimp, wild-caught, peeled, deveined
- 2 tablespoons minced garlic
- 1 teaspoon onion powder
- 1 teaspoon basil
- 1 teaspoon ground black pepper
- 1/2 teaspoon dried oregano
- 2 tablespoons olive oil
- 2/3 cup grated parmesan cheese, reduced Fat
- 2 tablespoons lemon juice

Directions:

- Switch on the air fryer, insert fryer basket, grease it with olive oil, then shut with its lid, set the fryer at 350 degrees F and preheat for 5 minutes
- Meanwhile, place cheese in a bowl, add remaining ingredients except for shrimps and lemon juice and stir until combined.
- Add shrimps and then toss until well coated.
- Open the fryer, add shrimps in it, spray oil over them, close with its lid and cook for 10 minutes until nicely golden and crispy, shaking halfway through the frying.
- When air fryer beeps, open its lid, transfer chicken onto a serving plate, Drizzle with lemon juice and serve.

120) Fish Sticks

Preparation Time: 5 minutes

Cooking Time: 15 minutes

Servings: 4

Nutrition: Calories 263 Cal Carbs 1g Fat 16g Protein 26.4g

Ingredients:

- 1-pound cod, wild-caught
- ½ teaspoon ground black pepper
- 3/4 teaspoon Cajun seasoning
- 1 teaspoon salt
- 1 1/2 cups pork rind
- 1/4 cup mayonnaise, reduced Fat
- 2 tablespoons water
- 2 tablespoons Dijon mustard

Directions:

- Switch on the air fryer, insert fryer basket, grease it with olive oil, then shut with its lid, set the fryer at 400 degrees F and preheat for 5 minutes
- Meanwhile, place mayonnaise in a bowl and then whisk in water and mustard until blended.
- Place pork rinds in a shallow dish, add Cajun seasoning, black pepper and salt and stir until mixed.
- Cut the cod into 1 by 2 inches pieces, then dip into mayonnaise mixture and then coat with pork rind mixture.
- Open the fryer; add fish sticks in it, spray with oil, close with its lid and cook for 10 minutes until nicely golden and crispy, flipping the sticks halfway through the frying.
- When air fryer beeps, open its lid, transfer fish sticks onto a serving plate and serve.

121) Shrimp with Lemon and Chile

Preparation Time: 5 minutes

Cooking Time: 12 minutes

Servings: 2

Nutrition: Calories 112.5 Cal Carbs 1g Fat 1g Protein 2g

Ingredients:

- 1-pound shrimp, wild-caught, peeled, deveined
- 1 lemon, sliced
- 1 small red chili pepper, sliced
- ½ teaspoon ground black pepper
- 1/2 teaspoon garlic powder
- 1 teaspoon salt
- 1 tablespoon olive oil

Directions:

- Switch on the air fryer, insert fryer basket, grease it with olive oil, then shut with its lid, set the fryer at 400 degrees F and preheat for 5 minutes
- Meanwhile, place shrimps in a bowl, add garlic, salt, black pepper, oil, and lemon slices and toss until combined.
- Open the fryer, add shrimps and lemon in it close with its lid and cook for 5 minutes, shaking halfway through the frying.
- Then add chili slices, shake the basket until mixed and continue cooking for 2 minutes or until shrimps are opaque and crispy.
- When air fryer beeps, open its lid, transfer shrimps and lemon slices onto a serving plate and serve.

122)   *Tilapia*

Preparation Time: 5 minutes

Cooking Time: 12 minutes

Servings: 2

Nutrition: Calories 36 Cal Carbs 0g Fat 0.75g Protein 7.4g

Ingredients:

- 2 tilapia fillets, wild-caught, 1 ½ inch thick
- 1 teaspoon old bay seasoning
- ¾ teaspoon lemon pepper seasoning
- ½ teaspoon salt

Directions:

- ❖ Switch on the air fryer, insert fryer basket, grease it with olive oil, then shut with its lid, set the fryer at 400 degrees F and preheat for 5 minutes
- ❖ Meanwhile, spray tilapia fillets with oil and then season with salt, lemon pepper, and old bay seasoning until evenly coated.
- ❖ Open the fryer, add tilapia in it, close with its lid and cook for 7 minutes until nicely golden and cooked, turning the fillets halfway through the frying.
- ❖ When air fryer beeps, open its lid, transfer tilapia fillets onto a serving plate and serve.

123)   *Tomato Basil Scallops*

Preparation Time: 5 minutes

Cooking Time: 15 minutes

Servings: 2

Nutrition: Calories 359 CalCarbs 6g Fat 33g Protein 9g

Ingredients:

- 8 jumbo sea scallops, wild-caught
- 1 tablespoon tomato paste
- 12 ounces frozen spinach, thawed and dry outed
- 1 tablespoon chopped fresh basil
- 1 teaspoon ground black pepper
- 1 teaspoon minced garlic
- 1 teaspoon salt
- 3/4 cup heavy whipping cream, reduced Fat

Directions:

- ❖ Switch on the air fryer, insert fryer basket, grease it with olive oil, then shut with its lid, set the fryer at 350 degrees F and preheat for 5 minutes
- ❖ Meanwhile, take a 7 inches baking pan, grease it with oil and place spinach in it in an even layer.
- ❖ Spray the scallops with oil, sprinkle with ½ teaspoon each of salt and black pepper and then place scallops over the spinach.
- ❖ Place tomato paste in a bowl, whisk in cream, basil, garlic, and remaining salt and black pepper until smooth, and then pour over the scallops.
- ❖ Open the fryer, place the pan in it, close with its lid and cook for 10 minutes until thoroughly cooked and sauce is hot.
- ❖ Serve straight away.

124)   *Shrimp Scampi*

Preparation Time: 5 minutes

Cooking Time: 12 minutes

Servings: 4

Nutrition: Calories 221 CalCarbs 1g Fat 13g Protein 23g

Ingredients:

- 1-pound shrimp, peeled, deveined
- 1 tablespoon minced garlic
- 1 tablespoon minced basil
- 1 tablespoon lemon juice
- 1 teaspoon dried chives
- 1 teaspoon dried basil
- 2 teaspoons red pepper flakes
- 4 tablespoons butter, unsalted
- 2 tablespoons chicken stock

Directions:

- ❖ Switch on the air fryer, insert fryer pan, grease it with olive oil, then shut with its lid, set the fryer at 330 degrees F and preheat for 5 minutes
- ❖ Add butter in it along with red pepper and garlic and cook for 2 minutes or until the butter has melted.
- ❖ Then add remaining ingredients in the pan, stir until mixed and continue cooking for 5 minutes until shrimps have cooked, stirring halfway through.
- ❖ When done, remove the pan from the air fryer, stir the shrimp scampi, let it rest for 1 minute and then stir again.
- ❖ Garnish shrimps with basil leaves and serve.

125)   *Salmon Cakes*

Preparation Time: 5 minutes

Cooking Time: 12 minutes

Servings: 2

Nutrition: Calories 517 CalCarbs 15g Fat 27g Protein 52g

Ingredients:

- ½ cup almond flour
- 15 ounces cooked pink salmon
- ¼ teaspoon ground black pepper
- 2 teaspoons Dijon mustard
- 2 tablespoons chopped fresh dill
- 2 tablespoons mayonnaise, reduced Fat
- 1 egg, pastured
- 2 wedges of lemon

Directions:

- ❖ ½ cup almond flour
- ❖ 15 ounces cooked pink salmon
- ❖ ¼ teaspoon ground black pepper
- ❖ 2 teaspoons Dijon mustard
- ❖ 2 tablespoons chopped fresh dill
- ❖ 2 tablespoons mayonnaise, reduced Fat
- ❖ 1 egg, pastured
- ❖ 2 wedges of lemon

126) *Cilantro Lime Shrimps*

Preparation Time: 25 minutes

Cooking Time: 21 minutes

Servings: 4

Nutrition: Calories 59 Cal Carbs 0.3g Fat 1.5g Protein 11g

Ingredients:

- 1/2-pound shrimp, peeled, deveined
- 1/2 teaspoon minced garlic
- 1 tablespoon chopped cilantro
- 1/2 teaspoon paprika
- ¾ teaspoon salt
- 1/2 teaspoon ground cumin
- 2 tablespoons lemon juice

Directions:

- ❖ Take 6 wooden skewers and let them soak in warm water for 20 minutes
- ❖ Meanwhile, switch on the air fryer, insert fryer basket, grease it with olive oil, then shut with its lid, set the fryer at 350 degrees F and let preheat.
- ❖ Whisk together lemon juice, paprika, salt, cumin, and garlic in a large bowl, then add shrimps and toss until well coated.
- ❖ Dry out the skewers and then thread shrimps in them.
- ❖ Open the fryer, add shrimps in it in a single layer, spray oil over them, close with its lid and cook for 8 minutes until nicely golden and cooked, turning the skewers halfway through the frying.
- ❖ When air fryer beeps, open its lid, transfer shrimps onto a serving plate and keep them warm.
- ❖ Cook remaining shrimp skewers in the same manner and serve.

127) *Cajun Style Shrimp*

Preparation Time: 3 minutes

Cooking Time: 10 minutes

Servings: 2

Nutrition: Calories 126 Fat 6g Carbs 2g Proteins: 33g

Ingredients:

- 6g of salt
- 2g smoked paprika
- 2ggarlic powder
- 2g Italian seasoning
- 2g chili powder
- 1g onion powder
- 1g cayenne pepper
- 1g black pepper
- 1g dried thyme
- 454g large shrimp, peeled and unveiled
- 30 ml of olive oil
- Lime wedges, to serve

Directions:

- ❖ Select Preheat, in the air fryer, set the temperature to 190°C and press Start/Pause. Combine all seasonings in a large bowl. Set aside
- ❖ Mix the shrimp with olive oil until they are evenly coated. Sprinkle the dressing mixture over the shrimp and stir until well coated. Place the shrimp in the preheated air fryer.
- ❖ Select Shrimp set the time to 5 minutes and press Start/Pause. Shake the baskets in the middle of cooking.Serve with pieces of lime.

128) *Tuna Pie*

Preparation Time: 10 minutes

Cooking Time: 30 minutes

Servings: 4

Nutrition: Calories 244 Fat 13.67g Carbs 21.06g Protein 8.72g

Ingredients:

- 2 hard-boiled eggs
- 2 tuna cans
- 200 ml fried tomato
- 1 sheet of broken dough

Directions:

- ❖ Cut the eggs into small pieces and mix with the tuna and tomato.
- ❖ Spread the sheet of broken dough and cut into two equal squares.
- ❖ Put the mixture of tuna, eggs, and tomato on one of the squares.
- ❖ Cover with the other, join at the ends and decorate with leftover little pieces.
- ❖ Preheat the air fryer a few minutes at 1800C.
- ❖ Enter in the air fryer basket and set the timer for 15 minutes at 1800C

AIR FRYER
DINNER RECIPE

129) *Buttermilk Marinated Chicken*

Preparation Time: 10 minutes

Cooking Time: 25 minutes

Servings: 6

Nutrition: Calories 284 Fat 7.9 g Carbs 46 g Protein 17.9 g

Ingredients:

- 3-lb. whole chicken
- 1 tablespoon salt
- 1-pint buttermilk

Directions:

- ❖ Place the whole chicken in a large bowl and Drizzle with salt on top.
- ❖ Pour the buttermilk over it and leave the chicken soaked overnight.
- ❖ Cover the chicken bowl and refrigerate overnight.
- ❖ Remove the chicken from the marinade and fix it on the rotisserie rod in the Air fryer oven.
- ❖ Turn the dial to select the "Air Roast" mode.
- ❖ Hit the Time button and again use the dial to set the cooking time to 25 minutes
- ❖ Now push the Temp button and rotate the dial to set the temperature at 370 degrees F.
- ❖ Close its lid and allow the chicken to roast.
- ❖ Serve warm.

130) *Thyme Turkey Breast*

Preparation Time: 10 minutes

Cooking Time: 40 minutes

Servings: 4

Nutrition: Calories 334 Fat 4.7 g Carbs 54.1 g Protein 26.2 g

Ingredients:

- 2 lb. turkey breast
- Salt, to taste
- Black pepper, to taste
- 4 tablespoon butter, melted
- 3 cloves garlic, minced
- 1 teaspoon thyme, chopped
- 1 teaspoon rosemary, chopped

Directions:

- ❖ Mix butter with salt, black pepper, garlic, thyme, and rosemary in a bowl.
- ❖ Rub this seasoning over the turkey breast liberally and place in the Air Fryer basket.
- ❖ Turn the dial to select the "Air Fry" mode.
- ❖ Hit the Time button and again use the dial to set the cooking time to 40 minutes
- ❖ Now push the Temp button and rotate the dial to set the temperature at 375 degrees F.
- ❖ Once preheated, place the Air fryer basket inside the oven
- ❖ Slice and serve fresh.

131) *Roasted Duck*

Preparation Time: 10 minutes

Cooking Time: 3 hours

Servings: 12

Nutrition: Calories 387 Fat 6 g Carbs 37.4 g Protein 14.6 g

Ingredients:

- 6 lb. whole Pekin duck
- Salt
- 5 garlic cloves chopped
- 1 lemon, chopped
- Glaze
- 1/2 cup balsamic vinegar
- 1 lemon, juiced
- 1/4 cup honey

Directions:

- ❖ Place the Pekin duck in a baking tray and add garlic, lemon, and salt on top.
- ❖ Whisk honey, vinegar, and honey in a bowl.
- ❖ Brush this glaze over the duck liberally.
- ❖ Marinate overnight in the refrigerator.
- ❖ Remove the duck from the marinade and fix it on the rotisserie rod in the
- ❖ Air fryer oven
- ❖ Turn the dial to select the "Air Roast" mode.
- ❖ Hit the Time button and again use the dial to set the cooking time to 3 hours.
- ❖ Now push the Temp button and rotate the dial to set the temperature at 350 degrees F.
- ❖ Close its lid and allow the duck to roast.
- ❖ Serve warm.

132) Chicken Drumsticks

Preparation Time: 10 minutes

Cooking Time: 20 minutes

Servings: 8

Nutrition: Calories 212 Fat 11.8 g Carbs 14.6 g Protein 17.3 g

Ingredients:

- 8 chicken drumsticks
- 2 tablespoon olive oil
- 1 teaspoon salt
- 1 teaspoon pepper
- 1 teaspoon garlic powder
- 1 teaspoon paprika
- 1/2 teaspoon cumin

Directions:

- ❖ Mix olive oil with salt, black pepper, garlic powder, paprika, and cumin in a bowl.
- ❖ Rub this mixture liberally over all the drumsticks.
- ❖ Place these drumsticks in the Air fryer basket.
- ❖ Turn the dial to select the "Air Fry" mode.
- ❖ Hit the Time button and again use the dial to set the cooking time to 20 minutes
- ❖ Now push the Temp button and rotate the dial to set the temperature at 375 degrees F.
- ❖ Once preheated, place the Air fryer basket inside the oven.
- ❖ Flip the drumsticks when cooked halfway through.
- ❖ Resume air frying for another rest of the 10 minutes
- ❖ Serve warm.

133) Blackened Chicken Bake

Preparation Time: 10 minutes

Cooking Time: 18 minutes

Servings: 4

Nutrition: Calories 412 Fat 24.8 g Carbs 43.8 g Protein 18.9 g

Ingredients:

- 4 chicken breasts
- 2 teaspoon olive oil
- Seasoning:
- 1 1/2 tablespoon brown sugar
- 1 teaspoon paprika
- 1 teaspoon dried oregano
- 1/4 teaspoon garlic powder
- 1/2 teaspoon salt and pepper
- Garnish:
- Chopped parsley

Directions:

- ❖ Mix olive oil with brown sugar, paprika, oregano, garlic powder, salt, and black pepper in a bowl.
- ❖ Place the chicken breasts in the baking tray of the Ninja Oven.
- ❖ Pour and rub this mixture liberally over all the chicken breasts.
- ❖ Turn the dial to select the "Bake" mode.
- ❖ Hit the Time button and again use the dial to set the cooking time to 18 minutes
- ❖ Now push the Temp button and rotate the dial to set the temperature at 425 degrees F.
- ❖ Once preheated, place the baking tray inside the oven
- ❖ Serve warm.

134) Crusted Chicken Drumsticks

Preparation Time: 10 minutes

Cooking Time: 10 minutes

Servings: 4

Nutrition: Calories 331 Fat 2.5 g Carbs 69 g Protein 28.7g

Ingredients:

- 1 lb. chicken drumsticks
- 1/2 cup buttermilk
- 1/2 cup panko breadcrumbs
- 1/2 cup flour
- 1/4 teaspoon baking powder
- Spice Mixture:
- 1/2 teaspoon salt
- 1/2 teaspoon celery salt
- 1/4 teaspoon oregano
- 1/4 teaspoon cayenne
- 1 teaspoon paprika
- 1/4 teaspoon garlic powder
- 1/4 teaspoon dried thyme
- 1/2 teaspoon ground ginger
- 1/2 teaspoon white pepper
- 1/2 teaspoon black pepper
- 3 tablespoon butter melted

Directions:

- ❖ Soak chicken in the buttermilk and cover to marinate overnight in the refrigerator. Mix spices with flour, breadcrumbs, and baking powder in a shallow tray. Remove the chicken from the milk and coat them well with the flour spice mixture
- ❖ Place the chicken drumsticks in the Air fryer basket of the Ninja Oven.
- ❖ Pour the melted butter over the drumsticks
- ❖ Turn the dial to select the "Air fry" mode. Hit the Time button and again use the dial to set the cooking time to 10 minutes Now push the Temp button and rotate the dial to set the temperature at 425 degrees F.
- ❖ Once preheated, place the baking tray inside the oven
- ❖ Flip the drumsticks and resume cooking for another 10 minutes
- ❖ Serve warm.

135) _Roasted Turkey Breast_

Preparation Time: 10 minutes

Cooking Time: 50 minutes

Servings: 6

Nutrition: Calories 322 Fat 11.8 Carbs 14.6 g Protein 17.3 g

Ingredients:

- 3 lb. boneless turkey breast
- ¼ cup mayonnaise
- 2 teaspoon poultry seasoning
- 1 teaspoon salt
- ½ teaspoon garlic powder
- ¼ teaspoon black pepper

Directions:

- ❖ Whisk all the ingredients, including turkey in a bowl, and coat it well.
- ❖ Place the boneless turkey breast in the Air fryer basket.
- ❖ Rotate the dial to select the "Air fry" mode.
- ❖ Press the Time button and again use the dial to set the cooking time to 50 minutes
- ❖ Now press the Temp button and rotate the dial to set the temperature at 350 degrees F.
- ❖ Once preheated, place the air fryer basket in the Ninja oven and Close its lid to bake.
- ❖ Slice and serve.

136) _Brine Soaked Turkey_

Preparation Time: 10 minutes

Cooking Time: 45 minutes

Servings: 8

Nutrition: Calories 397 Fat 15.4 g Carbs 58.5 g Protein 7.9 g

Ingredients:

- 7 lb. bone-in, skin-on turkey breast
- Brine:
- 1/2 cup salt
- 1 lemon
- 1/2 onion
- 3 cloves garlic, smashed
- 5 sprigs fresh thyme
- 3 bay leaves
- Black pepper
- Turkey Breast:
- 4 tablespoon butter, softened
- 1/2 teaspoon black pepper
- 1/2 teaspoon garlic powder
- 1/4 teaspoon dried thyme
- 1/4 teaspoon dried oregano

Directions:

- ❖ Mix the turkey brine ingredients in a pot and soak the turkey in the brine overnight. Next day, remove the soaked turkey from the brine.
- ❖ Whisk the butter, black pepper, garlic powder, oregano, and thyme. Brush the butter mixture over the turkey then place it in a baking tray.
- ❖ Press "Power Button" of Air Fry Oven and turn the dial to select the "Air Roast" mode. Press the Time button and again turn the dial to set the cooking time to 45 minutes
- ❖ Now push the Temp button and rotate the dial to set the temperature at 370 degrees F. Once preheated, place the turkey baking tray in the oven and close its lid.
- ❖ Slice and serve warm.

137) _Turkey Meatballs_

Preparation Time: 10 minutes

Cooking Time: 20 minutes

Servings: 6

Nutrition: Calories 338 Fat 9.7 g Carbs 32.5 g Protein 10.3 g

Ingredients:

- 1.5 lb. turkey mince
- 1 red bell pepper, deseeded and chopped
- 1 large egg, beaten
- 4 tablespoons parsley, minced
- 1 tablespoon cilantro, minced
- Salt, to taste
- Black pepper, to taste

Directions:

- ❖ Toss all the meatball ingredients in a bowl and mix well. Make small meatballs out this mixture and place them in the air fryer basket.
- ❖ Press "Power Button" of Air Fry Oven and turn the dial to select the "Air Fry" mode. Press the Time button and again turn the dial to set the cooking time to 20 minutes
- ❖ Now push the Temp button and rotate the dial to set the temperature at 375 degrees F.Once preheated, place the air fryer basket inside and close its lid. Serve warm.

138) _Lemon Pepper Turkey_

Preparation Time: 10 minutes

Cooking Time: 45 minutes

Servings: 6

Nutrition: Calories 391 Fat 2.8 g Carbs 36.5 g Protein 6.6

Ingredients:

- 3 lbs. turkey breast
- 2 tablespoons oil
- 1 tablespoon Worcestershire sauce
- 1 teaspoon lemon pepper
- 1/2 teaspoon salt

Directions:

- ❖ Whisk everything in a bowl and coat the turkey liberally.
- ❖ Place the turkey in the Air fryer basket.
- ❖ Press "Power Button" of Air Fry Oven and turn the dial to select the "Air Fry" mode.
- ❖ Press the Time button and again turn the dial to set the cooking time to 45 minutes
- ❖ Now push the Temp button and rotate the dial to set the temperature at 375 degrees F.
- ❖ Once preheated, place the air fryer basket inside and close its lid.
- ❖ Serve warm.

139) Ground Chicken Meatballs

Preparation Time: 10 minutes

Cooking Time: 10 minutes

Servings: 4

Nutrition: Calories 453 Fat 2.4 g Carbs 18 g Protein 23.2 g

Ingredients:

- 1-lb. ground chicken
- 1/3 cup panko
- 1 teaspoon salt
- 2 teaspoons chives
- 1/2 teaspoon garlic powder
- 1 teaspoon thyme
- 1 egg

Directions:

- ❖ Toss all the meatball ingredients in a bowl and mix well. Make small meatballs out this mixture and place them in the air fryer basket.Press "Power Button" of Air Fry Oven and turn the dial to select the "Air Fry" mode. Press the Time button and again turn the dial to set the cooking time to 10 minutes
- ❖ Now push the Temp button and rotate the dial to set the temperature at 350 degrees F. Once preheated, place the air fryer basket inside and close its lid. Serve warm.

140) Parmesan Chicken Meatballs

Preparation Time: 10 minutes

Cooking Time: 12 minutes

Servings: 4

Nutrition: Calories 529 Fat 17 g Carbs 55 g Protein 41g

Ingredients:

- 1-lb. ground chicken
- 1 large egg, beaten
- ½ cup Parmesan cheese, grated
- ½ cup pork rinds, ground
- 1 teaspoon garlic powder
- 1 teaspoon paprika
- 1 teaspoon kosher salt
- ½ teaspoon pepper
- Crust:
- ½ cup pork rinds, ground

Directions:

- ❖ Toss all the meatball ingredients in a bowl and mix well. Make small meatballs out this mixture and roll them in the pork rinds.Place the coated meatballs in the air fryer basket. Press "Power Button" of Air Fry Oven and turn the dial to select the "Bake" mode.
- ❖ Press the Time button and again turn the dial to set the cooking time to 12 minutes. Now push the Temp button and rotate the dial to set the temperature at 400 degrees F.
- ❖ Once preheated, place the air fryer basket inside and close its lid.
- ❖ Serve warm.

141) Easy Italian Meatballs

Preparation Time: 10 minutes

Cooking Time: 13 minutes

Servings: 4

Nutrition: Calories 472 Fat 25.8 Carbs 1.7 g Protein 59.6 g

Ingredients:

- 2-lb. lean ground turkey
- ¼ cup onion, minced
- 2 cloves garlic, minced
- 2 tablespoons parsley, chopped
- 2 eggs
- 1½ cup parmesan cheese, grated
- ½ teaspoon red pepper flakes
- ½ teaspoon Italian seasoning
- Salt and black pepper to taste

Directions:

- ❖ Toss all the meatball ingredients in a bowl and mix well. Make small meatballs out this mixture and place them in the air fryer basket.
- ❖ Press "Power Button" of Air Fry Oven and turn the dial to select the "Air Fry" mode. Press the Time button and again turn the dial to set the cooking time to 13 minutes. Now push the Temp button and rotate the dial to set the temperature at 350 degrees F.
- ❖ Once preheated, place the air fryer basket inside and close its lid.Flip the meatballs when cooked halfway through.
- ❖ Serve warm.

142) Oregano Chicken Breast

Preparation Time: 10 minutes

Cooking Time: 25 minutes

Servings: 6

Nutrition: Calories 352 Fat 14 g Carbs: 15.8 g Protein 26 g

Ingredients:

- 2 lbs. chicken breasts, minced
- 1 tablespoon avocado oil
- 1 teaspoon smoked paprika
- 1 teaspoon garlic powder
- 1 teaspoon oregano
- 1/2 teaspoon salt
- Black pepper, to taste

Directions:

- ❖ Toss all the meatball ingredients in a bowl and mix well. Make small meatballs out this mixture and place them in the air fryer basket.
- ❖ Press "Power Button" of Air Fry Oven and turn the dial to select the "Air Fry" mode. Press the Time button and again turn the dial to set the cooking time to 25 minutes
- ❖ Now push the Temp button and rotate the dial to set the temperature at 375 degrees F.
- ❖ Once preheated, place the air fryer basket inside and close its lid.
- ❖ Serve warm.

143) _Lemon Chicken Breasts_

Preparation Time: 10 minutes

Cooking Time: 30 minutes

Servings: 4

Nutrition: Calories 388 Fat 8 g Carbs 8 g Protein 13 g

Ingredients:

- 1/4 cup olive oil
- 3 tablespoons garlic, minced
- 1/3 cup dry white wine
- 1 tablespoon lemon zest, grated
- 2 tablespoons lemon juice
- 1 1/2 teaspoons dried oregano, crushed
- 1 teaspoon thyme leaves, minced
- Salt and black pepper
- 4 skin-on boneless chicken breasts
- 1 lemon, sliced

Directions:

- ❖ Whisk everything in a baking pan to coat the chicken breasts well.
- ❖ Place the lemon slices on top of the chicken breasts.
- ❖ Spread the mustard mixture over the toasted bread slices.
- ❖ Press "Power Button" of Air Fry Oven and turn the dial to select the "Bake" mode.
- ❖ Press the Time button and again turn the dial to set the cooking time to 30 minutes
- ❖ Now push the Temp button and rotate the dial to set the temperature at 370 degrees F.
- ❖ Once preheated, place the baking pan inside and close its lid.
- ❖ Serve warm.

144) _Cajun Salmon_

Preparation Time: 5 minutes

Cooking Time: 10 minutes

Servings: 2

Nutrition: Calories 225 Carbs 0g Fat 10.5g Protein 22.1g

Ingredients:

- 2 Salmon steaks
- 2 tbsp cajun seasoning

Directions:

- ❖ Rub the salmon steaks with the Cajun seasoning evenly. Set aside for about 10 minutes. Arrange the salmon steaks onto the greased cooking tray. Arrange the drip pan in the bottom of the Instant Vortex Air Fryer Oven cooking chamber. Select "Air Fry" and then adjust the temperature to 390 °F. Set the time for 8 minutes and press "Start". When the display shows "Add Food" insert the cooking tray in the center position. When the display shows "Turn Food" turn the salmon steaks. When the cooking time is complete, remove the tray from the Vortex Oven. Serve hot.

145) _Buttered Salmon_

Preparation Time: 5 minutes

Cooking Time: 10 minutes

Servings: 2

Nutrition: Calories 276 Carbs 0g Fat 16.3g Protein 33.1g

Ingredients:

- 2 salmon fillets (6-oz)
- Salt and ground black pepper, as required
- 1 tbsp butter, melted

Directions:

- ❖ Season each salmon fillet with salt and black pepper and then, coat with the butter.
- ❖ Arrange the salmon fillets onto the greased cooking tray. Arrange the drip pan in the bottom of the Instant Vortex Air Fryer Oven cooking chamber.
- ❖ Select "Air Fry" and then adjust the temperature to 360 °F. Set the time for 10 minutes and press "Start".
- ❖ When the display shows "Add Food" insert the cooking tray in the center position.
- ❖ When the display shows "Turn Food" turn the salmon fillets.
- ❖ When cooking time is complete, remove the tray from the Vortex Oven. Serve hot.

146) *Crispy Tilapia*

Preparation Time: 5 minutes

Cooking Time: 15 minutes

Servings: 2

Nutrition: Calories 291 Carbs 4.9g Fat 14.6g Protein 34.8g

Ingredients:

- ¾ cup cornflakes, crushed
- 1 (1-oz.) packet, dry ranch-style dressing mix
- 2½ tbsp vegetable oil
- 2 eggs
- 4 (6-oz) tilapia fillets

Directions:

❖ In a shallow bowl, beat the eggs. In another bowl, add the cornflakes, ranch dressing, and oil and mix until a crumbly mixture form. Dip the fish fillets into egg and then, coat with the cornflake mixture.

❖ Arrange the tilapia fillets onto the greased cooking tray. Arrange the drip pan in the bottom of the Instant Vortex Air Fryer Oven cooking chamber. Select "Air Fry" and then adjust the temperature to 355 °F. Set the time for 14 minutes and press "Start".

❖ When the display shows "Add Food" insert the cooking tray in the center position. When the display shows "Turn Food" turn the tilapia fillets. When cooking time is complete, remove the tray from the Vortex Oven. Serve hot.

147) *Simple Haddock*

Preparation Time: 5 minutes

Cooking Time: 10 minutes

Servings: 2

Nutrition: Calories 251 Carbs 0g Fat 8.6g Protein 41.2g

Ingredients:

- 2 (6-oz) haddock fillets
- 1 tbsp olive oil
- Salt and ground black pepper, as required

Directions:

❖ Coat the haddock fillets with oil and then, sprinkle with salt and black pepper. Arrange the haddock fillets onto a greased cooking rack and spray with cooking spray.

❖ Arrange the drip pan in the bottom of the Instant Vortex Air Fryer Oven cooking chamber. Select "Air Fry" and then adjust the temperature to 355 °F. Set the time for 8 minutes and press "Start".

❖ When the display shows "Add Food" insert the cooking rack in the center position. When the display shows "Turn Food" do not turn food.

❖ When the cooking time is complete, remove the rack from the Vortex Oven. Serve hot.

148) *Crispy Haddock*

Preparation Time: 5 minutes

Cooking Time: 10 minutes

Servings: 3

Nutrition: Calories 456 Carbs 40.9g Fat 22.7g Protein 43.5g

Ingredients:

- ½ Cup flour
- ½ tsp. Paprika
- 1 egg, beaten
- ¼ cup mayonnaise
- 4 oz salt and vinegar potato chips, crushed finely
- 1 lb haddock fillet cut into 6 pieces

Directions:

❖ In a shallow dish, mix together the flour and paprika.

❖ In a second shallow dish, add the egg and mayonnaise and beat well. In a third shallow dish, place the crushed potato chips.

❖ Coat the fish pieces with flour mixture, then dip into egg mixture and finally coat with the potato chips.

❖ Arrange the fish pieces onto 2 cooking trays.

❖ Arrange the drip pan in the bottom of the Instant Vortex Air Fryer Oven cooking chamber.

❖ Select "Air Fry" and then adjust the temperature to 370 °F. Set the time for 10 minutes and press "Start".

❖ When the display shows "Add Food" insert 1 cooking tray in the top position and another in the bottom position.

❖ When the display shows "Turn Food" do not turn the food but switch the position of cooking trays.

❖ When cooking time is complete, remove the trays from the Vortex Oven. Serve hot.

149) Tuna Burgers

Preparation Time: 5 minutes

Cooking Time: 6 minutes

Servings: 4

Nutrition: Calories 151 Carbs 6.3g Fat 6.4g Protein 16.4g

Ingredients:

- 7 oz canned tuna
- 1 large egg
- ¼ cup breadcrumbs
- 1 tbsp. Mustard
- ¼ tsp garlic powder
- ¼ tsp onion powder
- ¼ tsp cayenne pepper
- Salt and ground black pepper, as required

Directions:

- ❖ Add all the ingredients into a bowl and mix until well combined. Make 4 equal-sized patties from the mixture.
- ❖ Arrange the patties onto a greased cooking rack. Arrange the drip pan in the bottom of the Instant Vortex Air Fryer Oven cooking chamber.
- ❖ Select "Air Fry" and then adjust the temperature to 400 °F. Set the time for 6 minutes and press "Start".
- ❖ When the display shows "Add Food" insert the cooking rack in the center position. When the display shows "Turn Food" turn the burgers.
- ❖ When the cooking time is complete, remove the tray from the Vortex Oven. Serve hot.

150) Crispy Prawns

Preparation Time: 5 minutes

Cooking Time: 10 minutes

Servings: 4

Nutrition: Calories 386 Carbs 36.1g Fat 17g Protein 21g

Ingredients:

- 1 egg
- ½ lb crushed nacho chips
- 12prawns, peeled and deveined

Directions:

- ❖ In a shallow dish, beat the egg. In another shallow dish, place the crushed nacho chips. Coat the prawn into egg and then roll into nacho chips.
- ❖ Arrange the coated prawns onto 2 cooking trays in a single layer. Arrange the drip pan in the bottom of the Instant Vortex Air Fryer Oven cooking chamber. Select "Air Fry" and then adjust the temperature to 355 °F. Set the time for 8 minutes and press "Start".
- ❖ When the display shows "Add Food" insert 1 tray in the top position and another in the bottom position. When the display shows "Turn Food" do not turn the food but switch the position of cooking trays. When cooking time is complete, remove the trays from the Vortex Oven. Serve hot.

151) Prawns in Butter Sauce

Preparation Time: 5 minutes

Cooking Time: 6 minutes

Servings: 2

Nutrition: Calories 189 Carbs 2.4g Fat 7.7g Protein 26g

Ingredients:

- ½ lb. Peeled and deveined large prawns
- 1 large garlic clove, minced
- 1 tbsp butter melted
- 1 tsp fresh lemon zest grated

Directions:

- ❖ Add all the ingredients into a bowl and toss to coat well. Set aside at room temperature for about 30 minutes. Arrange the prawn mixture into a baking dish that will fit in the Vortex Air Fryer Oven. Arrange the drip pan in the bottom of the Instant Vortex Air Fryer Oven cooking chamber. Select "Bake" and then adjust the temperature to 450 °F. Set the time for 6 minutes and press "Start".
- ❖ When the display shows "Add Food" insert the baking dish in the center position. When cooking time is complete, remove the baking dish from the Vortex Oven. When the display shows "Turn Food" do not turn food. When cooking time is complete, remove the baking dish from the Vortex Oven. Serve hot.

152) Air Fried Chicken Tenderloin

Preparation Time: 5 minutes

Cooking Time: 15 minutes

Servings: 8

Nutrition: Calories 130.3 Carbs0.7g Protein 8.7 g Fat 10.3 g

Ingredients:

- ½ cup almond flour
- 1 egg, beaten
- 2 tablespoons coconut oil
- 8 chicken tenderloins
- Salt and pepper to taste

Directions:

- ❖ Preheat the air fryer for 5 minutes Season the chicken tenderloin with salt and pepper to taste.
- ❖ Soak in beaten eggs then dredge in almond flour. Place in the air fryer and brush with coconut oil.
- ❖ Cook for 15 minutes at 3750F.
- ❖ Halfway through the cooking time, give the fryer basket a shake to cook evenly.

153) *Almond Flour Battered Chicken Cordon Bleu*

Preparation Time: 5 minutes

Cooking Time: 30 minutes

Servings: 2

Nutrition: Calories 1142 Carbs 5.5g Protein 79.4g Fat 89.1g

Ingredients:
- ¼ cup almond flour
- 1 slice cheddar cheese
- 1 slice of ham
- 1 small egg, beaten
- 1 teaspoon parsley
- 2 chicken breasts, butterflied
- Salt and pepper to taste

Directions:
- ❖ Season the chicken with parsley, salt and pepper to taste.
- ❖ Place the cheese and ham in the middle of the chicken and roll. Secure with toothpick.
- ❖ Soak the rolled-up chicken in egg and dredge in almond flour.
- ❖ Place in the air fryer.
- ❖ Cook for 30 minutes at 3500F.

154) *Almond Flour Coco-Milk Battered Chicken*

Preparation Time: 5 minutes

Cooking Time: 30 minutes

Servings: 4

Nutrition: Calories 590 Carbs 3.2g Protein 32.5 g Fat 38.6g

Ingredients:
- ¼ cup coconut milk
- ½ cup almond flour
- 1 ½ tablespoons old bay Cajun seasoning
- 1 egg, beaten
- 4 small chicken thighs
- Salt and pepper to taste

Directions:
- ❖ Preheat the air fryer for 5 minutes
- ❖ Mix the egg and coconut milk in a bowl.
- ❖ Soak the chicken thighs in the beaten egg mixture.
- ❖ In a mixing bowl, combine the almond flour, Cajun seasoning, salt and pepper.
- ❖ Dredge the chicken thighs in the almond flour mixture.
- ❖ Place in the air fryer basket.
- ❖ Cook for 30 minutes at 3500F.

155) *Bacon 'n Egg-Substitute Bake*

Preparation Time: 5 minutes

Cooking Time: 30 minutes

Servings: 4

Nutrition: Calories 459

Carbs 21.0g

Protein 29.4g

Fat 28.5g

Ingredients:
- 1 (6 ounce) package Canadian bacon, quartered
- 1/2 cup 2% milk
- 1/4 teaspoon ground mustard
- 1/4 teaspoon salt
- 2 cups shredded Cheddar-Monterey Jack cheese blend
- 3/4 cup and 2 tablespoons egg substitute (such as Egg Beaters® Southwestern Style)
- 4 frozen hash brown patties

Directions:
- ❖ Lightly grease baking pan of air fryer with cooking spray.
- ❖ Evenly spread hash brown patties on bottom of pan. Top evenly with bacon and then followed by cheese.
- ❖ In a bowl, whisk well mustard, salt, milk, and egg substitute. Pour over bacon mixture.
- ❖ Cover air fryer baking pan with foil.
- ❖ Preheat air fryer to 330oF.
- ❖ Cook for another 20 minutes, remove foil and continue cooking for another 15 minutes or until eggs are set.
- ❖ Serve and enjoy.

156) *Basil-Garlic Breaded Chicken Bake*

Preparation Time: 5 minute

Cooking Time: 30 minutes

Servings: 2

Nutrition: Calories 311 Carbs 22.0g Protein 31.0g Fat 11.0g

Ingredients:
- 2 boneless skinless chicken breast halves (4 ounces each)
- 1 tablespoon butter, melted
- 1 large tomato, seeded and chopped
- 2 garlic cloves, minced
- 1 1/2 tablespoons minced fresh basil
- 1/2 tablespoon olive oil
- 1/2 teaspoon salt
- 1/4 cup all-purpose flour
- 1/4 cup egg substitute
- 1/4 cup grated Parmesan cheese
- 1/4 cup dry bread crumbs
- 1/4 teaspoon pepper

Directions:
- ❖ In shallow bowl, whisk well egg substitute and place flour in a separate bowl. Dip chicken in flour, then egg, and then flour. In a small bowl whisk well the butter, bread crumbs and cheese. Sprinkle over chicken.
- ❖ Lightly grease baking pan of air fryer with cooking spray. Place breaded chicken on bottom of pan. Cover with foil.
- ❖ For 20 minutes, cook it on 390 F.
- ❖ Meanwhile, in a bowl whisk well remaining ingredient.
- ❖ Remove foil from pan and then pour over chicken the remaining ingredients.
- ❖ Cook for 8 minutes
- ❖ Serve and enjoy.

157) BBQ Chicken Recipe from Greece

Preparation Time: 5 minutes

Cooking Time: 24minutes

Servings: 2

Nutrition: Calories 242 Carbs 12.3g Protein 31.0g Fat 7.5g

Ingredients:

- 1 (8 ounce) container fat-free plain yogurt
- 2 tablespoons fresh lemon juice
- 2 teaspoons dried oregano
- 1-pound skinless, boneless chicken breast halves - cut into 1-inch pieces
- 1 large red onion, cut into wedges
- 1/2 teaspoon lemon zest
- 1/2 teaspoon salt
- 1 large green bell pepper, cut into 1 1/2-inch pieces
- 1/3 cup crumbled feta cheese with basil and sun-dried tomatoes
- 1/4 teaspoon ground black pepper
- 1/4 teaspoon crushed dried rosemary

Directions:

- ❖ In a shallow dish, mix well rosemary, pepper, salt, oregano, lemon juice, lemon zest, feta cheese, and yogurt. Add chicken and toss well to coat. Marinate in the ref for 3 hours.
- ❖ Thread bell pepper, onion, and chicken pieces in skewers. Place on skewer rack.
- ❖ For 12 minutes, cook it on 360oF. Turnover skewers halfway through cooking time. If needed, cook in batches.
- ❖ Serve and enjoy.

158) BBQ Pineapple 'n Teriyaki Glazed Chicken

Preparation Time: 5 minutes

Cooking Time: 20 minutes

Servings: 2

Nutrition: Calories 391 Carbs 58.7g Protein 31.2g Fat 3.4g

Ingredients:

- ¼ cup pineapple juice
- ¼ teaspoon pepper
- ½ cup brown sugar
- ½ cup soy sauce
- ½ teaspoon salt
- 1 green bell pepper, cut into 1-inch cubes
- 1 red bell pepper, cut into 1-inch cubes
- 1 red onion, cut into 1-inch cubes
- 1 Tablespoon cornstarch
- 1 Tablespoon water
- 1 yellow red bell pepper, cut into 1-inch cubes
- 2 boneless skinless chicken breasts cut into 1-inch cubes
- 2 cups fresh pineapple cut into 1-inch cubes
- 2 garlic cloves, minced
- Green onions, for garnish

Directions:

- ❖ In a saucepan, bring to a boil salt, pepper, garlic, pineapple juice, soy sauce, and brown sugar. In a small bowl whisk well, cornstarch and water. Slowly stir in to mixture in pan while whisking constantly. Simmer until thickened, around 3 minutes. Save ¼ cup of the sauce for basting and set aside.
- ❖ In shallow dish, mix well chicken and remaining thickened sauce. Toss well to coat. Marinate in the ref for a half hour.
- ❖ Thread bell pepper, onion, pineapple, and chicken pieces in skewers. Place on skewer rack in air fryer.
- ❖ For 10 minutes, cook on 360oF. Turnover skewers halfway through cooking time. and baste with sauce. If needed, cook in batches.
- ❖ Serve and enjoy with a sprinkle of green onions.

159) BBQ Turkey Meatballs with Cranberry Sauce

Preparation Time: 5 minutes

Cooking Time: 20 minutes

Servings: 4

Nutrition: Calories 217 Carbs 11.5g Protein 28.0g Fat 10.9g

Ingredients:

- 1 ½ tablespoons of water
- 2 teaspoons cider vinegar
- 1 tsp. salt and more to taste
- 1-pound ground turkey
- 1 1/2 tablespoons barbecue sauce
- 1/3 cup cranberry sauce
- 1/4-pound ground bacon

Directions:

- ❖ In a bowl, mix well with hands the turkey, ground bacon and a tsp. of salt. Evenly form into 16 equal sized balls.
- ❖ In a small saucepan boil cranberry sauce, barbecue sauce, water, cider vinegar, and a dash or two of salt. Mix well and simmer for 3 minutes
- ❖ Thread meatballs in skewers and baste with cranberry sauce. Place on skewer rack in air fryer.
- ❖ For 15 minutes, cook it on 360oF. Every after 5 minutes of cooking time, turnover skewers and baste with sauce. If needed, cook in batches.
- ❖ Serve and enjoy.

160) *Blueberry Overload French Toast*

Preparation Time: 5 minutes

Cooking Time: 40 minutes

Servings: 5

Nutrition: Calories 492 Carbs 51.9g Protein 15.1g Fat 24.8g

Ingredients:

- 1 (8 ounce) package cream cheese, cut into 1-inch cubes
- 1 cup fresh blueberries, divided
- 1 cup milk
- 1 tablespoon cornstarch
- 1/2 cup water
- 1/2 cup white sugar
- 1/2 teaspoon vanilla extract
- 1-1/2 teaspoons butter
- 2 tablespoons and 2 teaspoons maple syrup
- 6 eggs, beaten
- 6 slices day-old bread, cut into 1-inch cubes

Directions:

- ❖ Lightly grease baking pan of air fryer with cooking spray.
- ❖ Evenly spread half of the bread on bottom of pan. Sprinkle evenly the cream cheese and ½ cup blueberries. Add remaining bread on top.
- ❖ In a large bowl, whisk well eggs, milk, syrup, and vanilla extract. Pour over bread mixture.
- ❖ Cover air fryer baking pan with foil and refrigerate overnight.
- ❖ Preheat air fryer to 330oF.
- ❖ Cook for 25 minutes covered in foil, remove foil and cook for another 20 minutes or until middle is set.
- ❖ Meanwhile, make the sauce by mixing cornstarch, water, and sugar in a saucepan and bring to a boil. Stir in remaining blueberries and simmer until thickened and blueberries have burst.
- ❖ Serve and enjoy with blueberry syrup.

161) *Broccoli-Rice 'n Cheese Casserole*

Preparation Time: 5 minutes

Cooking Time: 30 minutes

Servings: 4

Nutrition: Calories 752 Carbs 82.7g Protein 36.0g Fat 30.8g

Ingredients:

- 1 (10 ounce) can chunk chicken, Dry out
- 1 cup uncooked instant rice
- 1 cup water
- 1/2 (10.75 ounce) can condensed cream of chicken soup
- 1/2 (10.75 ounce) can condensed cream of mushroom soup
- 1/2 cup milk
- 1/2 small white onion, chopped
- 1/2-pound processed cheese food
- 2 tablespoons butter
- 8-ounce frozen chopped broccoli

Directions:

- ❖ Lightly grease baking pan of air fryer with cooking spray.
- ❖ Add water and bring to a boil at 390oF. Stir in rice and cook for 3 minutes. Stir in processed cheese, onion, broccoli, milk, butter, chicken soup, mushroom soup, and chicken.
- ❖ Mix well. Cook for 15 minutes at 390oF, fluff mixture and continue cooking for another 10 minutes until tops are browned.
- ❖ Serve and enjoy.

162) *Buffalo Style Chicken Dip*

Preparation Time: 5 minutes

Cooking Time: 10 minutes

Servings: 4

Nutrition: Calories 405 Carbs 3.2g Protein 17.1g Fat 35.9g

Ingredients:

- 1 (8 ounce) package cream cheese, softened
- 1 tablespoon shredded pepper Jack cheese
- 1/2 pinch cayenne pepper, for garnish
- 1/2 pinch cayenne pepper, or to taste
- 1/4 cup and 2 tablespoons hot pepper sauce (such as Frank's Reshoot®)
- 1/4 cup blue cheese dressing
- 1/4 cup crumbled blue cheese
- 1/4 cup shredded pepper Jack cheese
- 1/4 teaspoon seafood seasoning (such as Old Bay®)
- 1-1/2 cups diced cooked rotisserie chicken

Directions:

- ❖ Lightly grease baking pan of air fryer with cooking spray.
- ❖ Mix in cayenne pepper, seafood seasoning, crumbled blue cheese, blue cheese dressing, pepper Jack, hot pepper sauce, cream cheese, and chicken.
- ❖ For 15 minutes, cook it on 390 F.
- ❖ Let it stand for 5 minutes and garnish with cayenne pepper.
- ❖ Serve and enjoy.

163) _Buttered Spinach-Egg Omelet_

Preparation Time: 5 minutes

Cooking Time: 10 minutes

Servings: 4

Nutrition:

Ingredients:
- ¼ cup coconut milk
- 1 tablespoon melted butter
- 1-pound baby spinach, chopped finely
- 3 tablespoons olive oil
- 4 eggs, beaten
- Salt and pepper to taste

Directions:
- ¼ cup coconut milk
- 1 tablespoon melted butter
- 1-pound baby spinach, chopped finely
- 3 tablespoons olive oil
- 4 eggs, beaten
- Salt and pepper to taste

164) _Caesar Marinated Grilled Chicken_

Preparation Time: 5 minutes

Cooking Time: 20 minutes

Servings: 3

Nutrition: Calories 339 Carbs 9.5g Protein 32.6g Fat 18.9g

Ingredients:
- ¼ cup crouton
- 1 teaspoon lemon zest. Form into ovals, skewer and grill.
- 1/2 cup Parmesan
- 1/4 cup breadcrumbs
- 1-pound ground chicken
- 2 tablespoons Caesar dressing and more for drizzling
- 2-4 romaine leaves

Directions:
- In a shallow dish, mix well chicken, 2 tablespoons Caesar dressing, parmesan, and breadcrumbs. Mix well with hands. Form into 1-inch oval patties.
- Thread chicken pieces in skewers. Place on skewer rack in air fryer.
- For 12 minutes, cook it on 360oF. Turnover skewers halfway through cooking time. If needed, cook in batches.
- Serve and enjoy on a bed of lettuce and sprinkle with croutons and extra dressing.

165) _Cheese Stuffed Chicken_

Preparation Time: 5 minutes

Cooking Time: 25 minutes

Servings: 4

Nutrition: Calories 727 Carbs 5.4 g Protein 73.1g Fat 45.9g

Ingredients:
- 1 tablespoon creole seasoning
- 1 tablespoon olive oil
- 1 teaspoon garlic powder
- 1 teaspoon onion powder
- 4 chicken breasts, butterflied and pounded
- 4 slices Colby cheese
- 4 slices pepper jack cheese

Directions:
- Preheat the air fryer to 3900F.
- Place the grill pan accessory in the air fryer.
- Create the dry rub by mixing in a bowl the creole seasoning, garlic powder, and onion powder. Season it with salt and pepper if desired.
- Rub the seasoning on to the chicken.
- Place the chicken on a working surface and place a slice each of pepper jack and Colby cheese.
- Fold the chicken and secure the edges with toothpicks.
- Brush chicken with olive oil.
- Grill for 30 minutes and make sure to flip the meat every 10 minutes

166) _Cheeseburger Egg Rolls_

Preparation Time: 10 minutes

Cooking Time: 7 minutes

Servings: 6

Nutrition: Calories 153 Cal Fat 4 gCarbs 0 gProtein 12 g

Ingredients:
- 6 egg roll wrappers
- 6 chopped dill pickle chips
- 1 tbsp. yellow mustard
- 3 tbsp. cream cheese
- 3 tbsp. shredded cheddar cheese
- ½ C. chopped onion
- ½ C. chopped bell pepper
- ¼ tsp. onion powder
- ¼ tsp. garlic powder
- 8 ounces of raw lean ground beef

Directions:
- In a skillet, add seasonings, beef, onion, and bell pepper. Stir and crumble beef till fully cooked, and vegetables are soft.
- Take skillet off the heat and add cream cheese, mustard, and cheddar cheese, stirring till melted. Pour beef mixture into a bowl and fold in pickles.
- Lay out egg wrappers and place 1/6th of beef mixture into each one. Moisten egg roll wrapper edges with water. Fold sides to the middle and seal with water.
- Repeat with all other egg rolls.
- Place rolls into air fryer, one batch at a time.
- Pour into the Oven rack/basket. Place the Rack on the middle-shelf of the Air Fryer Oven. Set temperature to 392°F, and set time to 7 minutes

167) *Air Fried Grilled Steak*

Preparation Time: 5 minutes

Cooking Time: 45 minutes

Servings: 2

Nutrition: Calories 1536Fat 123.7 gCarbs 0 gProtein 103.4 g

Ingredients:

- 2 top sirloin steaks
- 3 tablespoons butter, melted
- 3 tablespoons olive oil
- Salt and pepper to taste

Directions:

- ❖ Preheat the Air Fryer Oven for 5 minutes. Season the sirloin steaks with olive oil, salt and pepper.
- ❖ Place the beef in the air fryer basket.
- ❖ Cook for 45 minutes at 350°F.
- ❖ Once cooked, serve with butter.

168) *Juicy Cheeseburgers*

Preparation Time: 5 minutes

Cooking Time: 15 minutes

Servings: 4

Nutrition: Calories 566 Cal Fat 39 gCarbs 0 gProtein 29 g

Ingredients:

- 1 pound 93% lean ground beef
- 1 teaspoon Worcestershire sauce
- 1 tablespoon burger seasoning
- Salt
- Pepper
- Cooking oil
- 4 slices cheese
- Buns

Directions:

- ❖ In a large bowl, mix the ground beef, Worcestershire, burger seasoning, and salt and pepper to taste until well blended.
- ❖ Spray the air fryer basket with cooking oil. You will need only a quick sprits. The burgers will produce oil as they cook. Shape the mixture into 4 patties.
- ❖ Place the burgers in the air fryer. The burgers should fit without the need to stack, but stacking is okay if necessary.
- ❖ Pour into the Oven rack/basket. Place the Rack on the middle-shelf of the Air Fryer Oven.
- ❖ Set temperature to 375°F, and set time to 8 minutes Cook for 8 minutes Open the air fryer and flip the burgers.
- ❖ Cook for an additional 3 to 4 minutes Check the inside of the burgers to determine if they have finished cooking.
- ❖ You can stick a knife or fork in the center to examine the color.
- ❖ Top each burger with a slice of cheese. Cook for an additional minute, or until the cheese has melted
- ❖ Serve on buns with any additional toppings of your choice.

169) *Spicy Thai Beef Stir-Fry*

Preparation Time: 15 minutes

Cooking Time: 9 minutes

Servings: 4

Nutrition: Calories 387 Cal Fat 22 gCarbs 0 gProtein 42 g

Ingredients:

- 1-pound sirloin steaks, thinly sliced
- 2 tablespoons lime juice, divided
- ⅓Cup crunchy peanut butter
- ½ cup beef broth
- 1 tablespoon olive oil
- 1½ cups broccoli florets
- 2 cloves garlic, sliced
- 1 to 2 red chili peppers, sliced

Directions:

- ❖ In a medium bowl, combine the steak with 1 tablespoon of the lime juice. Set aside.
- ❖ Combine the peanut butter and beef broth in a small bowl and mix well. Dry out the beef and add the juice from the bowl into the peanut butter mixture.
- ❖ In a 6-inch metal bowl, combine the olive oil, steak, and broccoli.
- ❖ Pour into the Oven rack/basket. Place the Rack on the middle-shelf of the Air Fryer Oven. Set temperature to 375°F, and set time to 4 minutes Cook for 3 to 4 minutes or until the steak is almost cooked and the broccoli is crisp and tender, shaking the basket once during cooking time.
- ❖ Add the garlic, chili peppers, and the peanut butter mixture and stir.
- ❖ Cook for 3 to 5 minutes or until the sauce is bubbling and the broccoli is tender.
- ❖ Serve over hot rice.

170) Beef Brisket Recipe from Texas

Preparation Time: 15 minutes

Cooking Time: 1 hour and 30 minutes

Servings: 8

Nutrition: Calories 306 Cal Fat 24.1 g Carbs 0 gProtein 18.3 g

Ingredients:

- 1 ½ cup beef stock
- 1 bay leaf
- 1 tablespoon garlic powder
- 1 tablespoon onion powder
- 2 pounds beef brisket, trimmed
- 2 tablespoons chili powder
- 2 teaspoons dry mustard
- 4 tablespoons olive oil
- Salt and pepper to taste

Directions:

- ❖ Preheat the Air Fryer Oven for 5 minutes Place all ingredients in a deep baking dish that will fit in the air fryer.
- ❖ Bake it for 1 hour and 30 minutes at 400°F.
- ❖ Stir the beef every after 30 minutes to soak in the sauce.

171) Copycat Taco Bell Crunch Wraps

Preparation Time: 10 minutes

Cooking Time: 2 minutes

Servings: 6

Nutrition: Calories 311 Cal Fat 9 gCarbs 0 gProtein 22 g

Ingredients:

- 6 wheat tostadas
- 2 C. sour cream
- 2 C. Mexican blend cheese
- 2 C. shredded lettuce
- 12 ounces low-sodium nacho cheese
- 3 Roma tomatoes
- 6 12-inch wheat tortillas
- 1 1/3 C. water
- 2 packets low-sodium taco seasoning
- 2 pounds of lean ground beef

Directions:

- ❖ Ensure your air fryer is preheated to 400 degrees.
- ❖ Make beef according to taco seasoning packets.
- ❖ Place 2/3 C. prepared beef, 4 tbsp. cheese, 1 tostada, 1/3 C. sour cream, 1/3 C. lettuce, 1/6th of tomatoes and 1/3 C. cheese on each tortilla.
- ❖ Fold up tortillas edges and repeat with remaining ingredients.
- ❖ Lay the folded sides of tortillas down into the air fryer and spray with olive oil.
- ❖ Set temperature to 400°F, and set time to 2 minutes Cook 2 minutes till browned.

172) Air Fryer Beef Casserole

Preparation Time: 5 minutes

Cooking Time: 30 minutes

Servings: 4

Nutrition: Calories 1520 Cal Fat 125.11 g Carbs 0 gProtein 87.9 g

Ingredients:

- 1 green bell pepper, seeded and chopped
- 1 onion, chopped
- 1-pound ground beef
- 3 cloves of garlic, minced
- 3 tablespoons olive oil
- 6 cups eggs, beaten
- Salt and pepper to taste

Directions:

- ❖ Preheat the Air Fryer Oven for 5 minutes
- ❖ In a baking dish that will fit in the air fryer, mix the ground beef, onion, garlic, olive oil, and bell pepper. Season it with salt and pepper to taste.
- ❖ Pour in the beaten eggs and give a good stir.
- ❖ Place the dish with the beef and egg mixture in the air fryer.
- ❖ Pour into the Oven rack/basket. Place the Rack on the middle-shelf of the Air Fryer Oven. Set temperature to 325°F, and set time to 30 minutes. Bake it for 30 minutes

173) Chimichurri Skirt Steak

Preparation Time: 10 minutes

Cooking Time: 8 minutes

Servings: 2

Nutrition: Calories 308.6 Cal Fat 22.6 gCarbs 3 gProtein 23.7 g

Ingredients:

- 2 x 8 oz. skirt steak
- 1 cup finely chopped parsley
- ¼ cup finely chopped mint
- 2 tbsp. fresh oregano (washed & finely chopped)
- 3 finely chopped cloves of garlic
- 1 tsp. red pepper flakes (crushed)
- 1 tbsp. ground cumin
- 1 tsp. cayenne pepper
- 2 tsp. smoked paprika
- 1 tsp. salt
- ¼ tsp. pepper
- ¾ cup oil
- 3 tbsp. red wine vinegar

Directions:

- ❖ Throw all the ingredients in a bowl (besides the steak) and mix well.
- ❖ Put ¼ cup of the mixture in a plastic baggie with the steak and leave in the fridge overnight (2–24hrs).
- ❖ Leave the bag out at room temperature for at least 30 min before popping into the air fryer.
- ❖ Preheat for a minute or two to 390° F before cooking until med–rare (8–10 min).
- ❖ Pour into the Oven rack/basket. Place the Rack on the middle-shelf of the Air Fryer Oven. Set temperature to 390°F, and set time to 10 minutes
- ❖ Put 2 Tbsp. of the chimichurri mix on top of each steak before serving.

6. Conclusion

Now what?

Now you are able to use your new air fryer in a full and thoroughly professional manner.

No more fatty and nasty food

No more losing time cooking

Now it's time for you to enjoy your kitchen creations each day, each week, all over the year!

I hope you all have enjoyed this cookbook

Happy eating!

By Brenda Roberts

CPSIA information can be obtained
at www.ICGtesting.com
Printed in the USA
BVHW052028300421
606133BV00013B/1967